BE STILL AND KNOW

BE STILL AND KNOW

GOD'S PRESENCE IN SILENCE

NORRIS J. CHUMLEY

Fortress Press
Minneapolis

BE STILL AND KNOW

God's Presence in Silence

Cover image © Norris J. Chumley
Cover design: Tory Herman

Library of Congress Cataloging-in-Publication Data

Print ISBN: 978-1-4514-7051-2

eBook ISBN: 978-1-4514-7991-1

The paper used in this publication meets the minimum requirements of American National Standard for Information Sciences — Permanence of Paper for Printed Library Materials, ANSI Z329.48-1984.

Manufactured in the U.S.A.

This book was produced using PressBooks.com, and PDF rendering was done by PrinceXML.

CONTENTS

Acknowledgements

This book is dedicated to God the Father, the Son, Jesus Christ, and the Holy Spirit. Thank you for my life and the ability to do your will.

I would like to thank my ancestors and family, my wife, Catherine Stine Chumley, sons Jack Hudson Morris Chumley and Nathaniel Buskirk Chumley, my sister, Ellen White Chumley, my brothers, Hays Hardesty Chumley and the late Gary Buskirk Chumley, and sister-in-law, Beth Baxter, brother-in-law, John Bower Stine III, and sister-in-law, Karen Heath Stine. I would also like to thank my father-in-law, the late Richard Dengler Stine, and mother-in-law, Dorothy Cornog Stine.

My colleague and friend, Janet R. Walton of Union Theological Seminary in New York City, has understood, believed in me, and championed my mission for many years. For this loyalty and assistance I am deeply appreciative.

Euan Cameron, Fr. John Chryssavgis, and the late George C. Stoney have been enormously helpful reviewing the content of this book, and in my doctoral studies. I have learned many things from their queries and comments, which have been incorporated into this text.

V. Rev. Dr. John McGuckin has been helpful to this project and inspired me to study early church history and asceticism.

Scott Cairns has been a valuable consultant. Ann Patrick Ware has been so thorough in assisting me with line editing.

I especially thank the Greek Orthodox Church, specifically His All Holiness Ecumenical Patriarch Bartholomew, Rev. Alexander Karloutsos, His Eminence Archbishop Demetrios, His Beatitude Patriarch Daniel Ciobotea, His Eminence Archbishop Damianos, and His Eminence Archbishop Iustinian.

I wish to thank the monastery leaders, the abbots and abbesses, hermits, monks, and nuns for participating in something new, and giving me great gifts of their trust and collegiality.

Harville Hendrix and Helen LaKelly Hunt encouraged me to return to school and deepen my knowledge. Their love and friendship have kept me going.

Finally, Todd Edison French and David Sanchez have been my close colleagues and friends. We have mutually encouraged each other and had a lot of fun in the process.

Preface

The purpose of the book is to analyze the ancient and contemporary practices of *silence* (*hesychia*, in Greek); second, to convey something of the personal religious experiences of monks and nuns using the practices today: through text, spoken direction, and instruction by example.

Some part of religious experience will always remain internal and impossible to convey in any medium. However, much about *silence* can be approached as an observable phenomenon through its different components: words and actions, images and sounds, textures and rituals, history and doctrine. Emotions and experiences cannot directly be seen or heard by others but may be secondarily represented by words, symbols, sounds, and images. Facial expressions, body positions, clothing, colors, textures, and so forth, may all help to express what words cannot fully describe, and they are important. The abstract ideas behind the experiences may be described in words and their associated meanings.

Silence or *Hesychia*,[1] a method of controlling the body and focusing the mind's attention with quietude and prayer in petition to Jesus Christ, is an ancient Orthodox Christian ascetic practice that can provide an opportunity for peace and a transcendent spiritual experience of God. According to some practitioners of *hesychia*, specifically the Athonites from the eleventh century on, the experience of God as transcendent "uncreated Light" has been likened to that of Christ's apostles witnessing his transfiguration on Mt. Tabor.[2]

---

1. Greek for "quietness" or "silence and stillness," originally signifying a state of withdrawal by ascetics for the purpose of contemplation; later a specific practice of prayer by Athonite monks, now a word that connotes a practice that is in use worldwide by Orthodox Christians and others.

2. As described in Saint Symeon the New Theologian, *The Practical and Theological Chapters & the Three Theological Discourses* (Kalamazoo, MI: Cistercian, 1982), 23.

With this book the internal, individual practice of *hesychia* has been documented and analyzed. Orthodox Christian monks and nuns in three original locations of *hesychia*—Egypt, Greece, and Romania—have intentionally chosen to offer commentary, descriptions, and demonstrations of their practices of *hesychia* to nonascetic Orthodox and secular audiences.

Hesychia originated when early Christians retreated to the solitude of the Egyptian desert in the second century. In the sixth century it was developed by monks at the monastery at Mt. Sinai Church of the Transfiguration, now also named "St. Catherine's Monastery." *The practice* became widely used in Christian Orthodox monasticism after the fourteenth century, particularly on Mt. Athos, and later spread to Eastern Europe and beyond among subsequent generations of monastic men and women. *Hesychia* became the primary element of eremitic[3] asceticism. It later found its way to coenobitic[4] and idiorrhythmic[5] communal practice, and it is still a primary contemplative method in monasteries in these locations and in monasteries throughout the world.

The goals of this book are to document and analyze: (1) the believed positive values of the practice of *hesychia* from the point of view of the practitioners, in antiquity and in the present, and (2) how the practice has historically been conveyed to others.

There have been numerous instructional texts and commentaries written on this subject.[6] There have been many films, too, on the

---

3. Solitary, individual ascetic practice, away from others.

4. Groups of two or more ascetics, assembled for the purpose of sharing meals, prayers, liturgy, etc.

5. Monks in community, but not necessarily sharing in group worship, prayer, work, or meals at the same time.

6. Many volumes exist in the form of primary source theological commentaries and dogma relevant to *hesychia*, cf. Origen (185–c. 254) *On First Principles, The Philokalia,* Macarius of Egypt (c. 300–391), *Homilies,* Evagrius (b. 399), *Gnostic Centuries* and *The Praktikos,* Diadochus (fifth century), *Gnostic Chapters,* John Climacus (525–606), *The Ladder of Divine Ascent,* Maximus the Confessor (580–662), *The Ascetic Life: The Four Centuries on Charity,* Symeon the New Theologian (949–1022), *On the Mystical Life: The Ethical Discourses,* Gregory of Sinai (1255–1346), *On Prayer,* Gregory Palamas (1296–1359), and notable analysis and commentary by Athanasius, Bradshaw, Brown, Chryssavgis, Florovsky, Harmless,

general topics of monasteries and monastic life, notably *Inside Mt. Athos* (BBC, 1970), *Frontline: The Early Christians* (WGBH/PBS, 2000), *Mt. Athos: Mountain of Silence* (Ministry of Hellenic Culture, 1989), *Into Great Silence* (feature film, 2006) and a CBS "60 Minutes" report on Mt. Athos (2011). As an additional component of my research, I made a feature documentary film, *Mysteries of the Jesus Prayer*, output from an ethnographic field study film, also titled "Be Still and Know," that features many of the practitioners in this book. It is widely available as a DVD and digital download, as well as a condensed one-hour version released on public television in the United States, and on SnagFilms.com. I have also had published a companion book to the feature film, on the making of the film and my personal experiences of *hesychia*.[7]

In this volume I will analyze the practice of silence, *hesychia*, its contemporary use and its historical origins, through research of selected ancient and contemporary texts,[8] secondary source criticism and analysis,[9] and utilization of modern techniques of interview, observation, and recording in high-definition digital film.[10]

To illustrate the use of *hesychia* in historical and contemporary contexts, I have visited each of the three locations where *hesychia* began and flourished: Egypt and the Sinai, Greece and Romania, using ancient texts, historical criticism, and personal interviews with contemporary *hesychasts* both in spoken/written words and in statements and actions.

Krivocheine, Lossky, Markides, McClellan, McGuckin, Merrill, Merton, Meyendorff, Migne, Papademetrio, Seraphim, Sherrard, Sophroni, Taft, Thunberg, Vasileios, Vivian, Waddell, Ward, Wybrew, et al.

7. For more information on the ethnographic film, feature documentary, and trade book, please visit www.JesusPrayerMovie.com.

8. Selected primary texts from ancient sources, biographies, doctrine, Liturgy of St. John Chrysostom, prayers, and pedagogical narratives will be utilized. See above, footnote 6.

9. See footnote 6 and Bibliography.

10. I have used a combination of ethnographic filming of intimate conversations with hermits, monks, and nuns, and documentary film exposition of the stated locations, churches, Byzantine works of art, voices, natural sounds, and prayer and liturgical services, both private and public.

Research into ancient texts is useful for analyzing both the history and the core of ascetic praxes, placing them into context in the eras in which they were written in order to understand the etymologies and to discern how *hesychia* was utilized in the past. The texts discussed in this book are well known, even legendary; they are the bases for ascetic praxes as well as the development of the church as well. The selected texts herein are all available in the English language; some are in multiple editions of translation, offering the possibility of further research and personal practice of concentrated prayer and *hesychia*.

In general, the texts are instruction manuals intended as spiritual and lifestyle guidance for monks and nuns. Their wisdom is not confined to the eras in which they are written, and their use beyond monasteries and convents may be fruitful.

The wisdom found in the ancient texts, and the rules for living prescribed by both ancient and contemporary practitioners, have stood the test of time for ample reason. They are intended as methods of seeking and communing with God, and as rules for living a life in dedication and obedience to God. These teachings have been useful, even salvific, for those who have followed them through the ages.

Yet, all of the teachings include recommendations for practicing *hesychia* and continual prayer under the guidance of a spiritual father or mother. None of them were intended for individual use without qualified guidance. Further, it important to understand that the ancient texts are for tonsured monastics, not laypersons. It is possible to integrate prayer and silent contemplation into one's life, but it is expressly not a good idea to attempt actual ascetic practices on one's own without proper guidance. Further, praxes of *hesychia* are always used in combination with the Holy Liturgy, ascetic rule, and specifically regular communion with God in the form of the Holy Mysteries: the Body and Blood of our Lord and Savior, Jesus Christ, known as the Holy Eucharist.

Finally, I've employed historical-critical analyses in all instances of ancient and contemporary asceticism throughout this book, attempting to contextualize the past with the present. It is of the essence to be aware of basic events in the eras in which the texts were conceived and recorded, as well as to draw contextual parallels to contemporary thinking and praxes. I encourage you to employ these methods in your further research and, if you so desire, to utilize what you discover in your own spiritual and religious praxes, and to seek qualified spiritual guidance.

Silence (*Hesychia*): A Method for Experiencing God

The practice of silence of the Greek, *hesychia*, the withdrawal from the external world with focus on inward stillness, contemplation, and prayer, and *hesychasm*, the later Athonite movement of prayer and bodily positioning in Orthodox monasticism, is a method of experiencing God predicated on the belief that a direct spiritual experience and union with God is possible. Long lines of *hesychasts*, from the second century to the present day, spoke and wrote about the fruits of their experiences.

Orthodox Christianity, by definition, preserves ancient beliefs and practices and is mostly unchanging. The Orthodox ascetic belief that communion with God may be achieved through the practices of individual retreat to silence and stillness and through continual prayer, individually or in community, in petition to Jesus Christ, is generally unchanged since its origins in the second century, but the method of how those beliefs and practices are conveyed to others has changed. This book argues and demonstrates how the transmission of *hesychia* has experienced change and innovation.

Implicit in the state and practices of *hesychia* is the importance of cessation of worldly conversation and activity in favor of a retreat into silence, stillness, and isolation. While within the practices of *hesychia* the relational experience of God-to-human being was held as paramount, the relationships of human-to-human are purposefully mitigated or avoided by monks: *hesychasts*, by tradition and as a rule, want to be left alone, preserve their state of *hesychia*, and/or only associate with other monks avoiding outside influences and disruptions. This attitude is particularly noticeable in the earliest known saints and practitioners. Today, there is a very strong insistence upon a relationship with a father/mother/elder, and the practice is considered nonviable if isolated from the Eucharistic life of the church, necessarily undertaken where "two or more are gathered" in the Holy Name of Jesus Christ.

The term *monk* or *monachos* itself means "one who is alone." This flight to solitude from the outer world was also a fleeing from other monks. But solitude and *hesychia* were not synonymous. The true goal was not just physical removal from stimuli or community pressures. It was what Harmless calls "a graced depth of inner stillness."[1] St. Joseph the Hesychast, a contemporary Athonite, wrote, "The aim was *hesychia*, quiet, the calm through the whole man that is like a still pool of water, capable of reflecting the sun. To be in true relationship with God, standing before him in every situation—that was the angelic life, the spiritual life, the monastic life, the aim and the way of the monk."[2] As Abba Alonius said, "Unless a man can say 'I alone and God are here,' he will not find the prayer of quiet."[3]

While *hesychia* has been taught through the ages by spiritual masters, it has historically been communicated on a one-to-one basis in monasteries only, either through a kind of mentor-protégé system or through the instructional texts of monastic manuals. So private is this practice that many nonascetic Orthodox remain entirely unaware of *hesychia*. Thus it is all the more unusual that a nonascetic, non-Orthodox scholar and ethnographer has been able to record both the praxes and instruction on text and on film to introduce them to a wider audience of both Orthodox and secular recipients.

The communications and experiences of the modern-day *hesychasts* through interviews and on film cannot be divorced from their historical, theological, and methodological contexts. Because the nature of these direct and mystical experiences of God is central to

1. William Harmless, *Desert Christians: An Introduction to the Literature of Early Monasticism* (Oxford: Oxford University Press, 2004), 228.

2. Benedicta Ward, *The Wisdom of the Desert Fathers: The Apophthegmata Patrum (the Anonymous Series)*, Fairacres Publication (Oxford: S. L. G., 1975), xvii.

3. Benedicta Ward, *The Sayings of the Desert Fathers: The Alphabetical Collection* (London: Mowbrays, 1975), Saying Number 1.

this research and essay, I will introduce the subject in Part One by analyzing and comparing the reports of actual experiences of God from the point of view of the key ancient practitioners. Part Two will present, analyze, and compare the stories, methodology, and pedagogy of contemporary and living spiritual masters, church officials, and practitioners of *hesychia*.

EXPERIENCES OF GOD

The question of whether it is truly possible to have a direct experience of God or a union with God or to see God is a central question of theology. It has been argued pro and con in the Bible and by ancient practitioners and modern scholars; yet in actuality it remains a timeless mystery. Eastern Orthodox ascetic doctrine today, as it has been filtered and interpreted over centuries of theory and practice, holds that God can indeed be known and experienced; the methodology of *hesychia* has developed and evolved to that end.

Hesychia and the word's associated derivatives—*hesychast* (a practitioner of *hesychia*) and *hesychasm* (the system and methodology *hesychasts* employ)—define and encompass several areas: a core idea and inner state; the practitioners who seek to attain that inner state; and the tradition of practices that has grown up around this desire. *Hesychia* describes a state of consciousness, one of peace and focus on God, the result of grace, practices of devoted prayer (mainly but not exclusively the Jesus Prayer), and partaking of the Holy Mysteries (the Eucharist) as well as management of physical, psychological, and intellectual aspects of the individual. *Hesychia* is not only silence and stillness as its description implies, but also an "attitude of listening to God and of openness towards Him" as described by Palmer, Sherrard, and Ware, the English-language editors of *The Philokalia*,[4] a later collection of mainly Athonite texts on the subject.

My survey of the history of *hesychia*, as revealed in primary and secondary sources, includes key theorists and practitioners who exemplified the experience of God and the attainment of *hesychia*

---

4. Nicodemus and Makarios, *The Philokalia: The Complete Text*, trans. G. E. H. Palmer, Philip Sherrard, and Kallistos Ware (London: Faber & Faber, 1979), 364.

through *hesychasm*. Conversations and formal ethnographic interviews and observation of living monks and *hesychasts* further reveal contemporary figures who, like their predecessors, stand out as ascetics who are filled with God's presence and possess high intellect—and who were also willing to leave seclusion for a moment to share their private experiences. I will begin by highlighting key attitudes and statements of ancient *hesychasts*. This purpose is twofold: first, to demonstrate the importance they assign to maintaining stillness, silence, and isolation from the world; second, to highlight some of the benefits of *hesychia*.

I also include admonishments and cautionary advice from master *hesychasts* for monks[5] to avoid or minimize contact with others (especially nonascetics and non-Orthodox) and to retain silence and stillness for the sake of preserving the traditions and practices, both individually and collectively. The departures from this silence and isolation that this thesis describes are only one of many paradoxes to be found in the analysis and conveyance of *hesychia* and *hesychasm*. It will be readily apparent to the reader how the values of *hesychasts* differ from those in the "outside" world: inner experiences are valued over external events, goals are spiritual not simply material, attention to one's own physical comfort is minimized in favor of obedience and service to God and other human beings. Awareness of those values will be important in understanding and putting into context the motivation of the monastics to consider the departure from "the world," and later the departure from tradition that the new transmission method described herein represents.

A Brief Historic Background to *Hesychia*

As *hesychia* is an ancient Orthodox Christian ascetic methodology that claims to provide an opportunity for peace and a transcendent spiritual experience of God in various forms and situations, it is assumed by practitioners that God can indeed be experienced.

---

5. The term "monk" in contemporary use in monasteries in Egypt, Greece, and Romania means a male renunciant. "Monastery" connotes a place for either male or female coenobitic ascetics.

According to Vladimir Lossky, the question of the experience of God in Orthodox practices of *hesychia* appears to have posed two variations: Is God's presence to be realized in some sort of life after death (in an eschatological or salvific sense), or may God be known in present, human life, in some sort of ecstatic or transcendent experience?[6] If the former is possible, is this vision or experience of God possible prior to death or at death itself? Or do we commune with God only after death and resurrection? In either case, is the union with God direct and personal or through an intermediary?

St. John wrote, "No one has seen the Father, except him who is with God; he has seen the Father,"[7] referring to Jesus Christ. The Synoptic Gospels recast the issue as not vision, but knowledge: "No one knows the Son, except the Father, and no one knows the Father except the Son and him to whom the Son chooses to reveal him."[8] In other words, divine knowledge can be given or shown to created humans by God the Father's Son, Jesus Christ.

The First Epistle of St. John[9] and St. Paul's Letter to the Corinthians[10] convey the promise of a vision of God associated with being sons of God, given by grace through love of the Father. This grace is not yet with us, as we of the world do not yet know God, because what we will be has not yet come. The fruit of his manifestation has not arrived. When he comes, we will be like him, and we will "see Him as He is." First and foremost, this revealing is for the followers of God, "the sons of God," or "children of God." Then, there is the element of eschatology, the final moment when God manifests, in the parousia, "when He will appear." Then, we will become "likenesses" of God, a product of God's divine grace and love. To Lossky, this is a causal relationship: "We shall be like him, for we shall see him as he is," a consequence of the vision of God. "The fact that we see God as He is shows that we are likenesses of Him."[11]

6. Vladimir Lossky, *The Vision of God*, trans. Ashleigh Moorhouse (London: Faith Press, 1963), 9–20.

7. John 6:46.

8. Cf. Matt. 11:27; Luke 10:22.

9. 3:1-2.

10. 13:12.

11. Lossky, *The Vision of God*, 25.

What do the early church fathers have to say on this matter? Specifically, how do they answer the question whether any vision of or union with God (however removed) can take place only after death or in the end time, or whether God may be known in the context of human life as we know it?

W. H. C. Frend asserts that Clement of Alexandria (c. 150–c. 215) also believed that we could become "likenesses" of God, not in an eschatological moment but through a process of lifelong purification, as the Platonists taught. Clement shared his philosophy with the Stoic and Christian law of purification and the superiority of virtue over reason; of us "making ready the way for him who is perfected in Christ . . . to prepare the way for the teaching that is royal in the highest sense of the word, by making men self-controlled, by molding character and making them ready to receive the truth."[12] Union with God, to become like God, was to become "free of the passions that hindered the soul's ascent to perfection and deification."[13] Attaining the likeness of God through gnosis (knowledge) was for a select few, but Clement wrote that God was accessible to those made ready by purification and the process of virtue. Through gnosis, the result of purification, we could experience "unity but beyond unity, transcending the monad," not through his creation, but through the Son or Word (Logos)—"his image, mind and reason, inseparable from Himself."[14] In other words, what we are able to commune with is not God but a reflection or incarnation of God rather than God's direct essence. Frend summarizes, "He (Christ) reflected God rather than contrasted with God, while the Spirit was light issuing from Him, to illuminate the faithful (through the prophets and philosophers) pervading the world and drawing him towards God."[15]

Moving beyond Scripture yet influenced by it, second-century authors St. Theophilus of Antioch and St. Irenaeus also speak of visions

---

12. Clement, *Stromateis*, trans. John Ferguson, vol. 1–3, Fathers of the Church (Washington, DC: Catholic University of America Press, 1991), I.16.80.6.

13. W. H. C. Frend, *The Rise of Christianity* (Philadelphia: Fortress Press, 1984), 370.

14. Clement, *Miscellanies*, trans. Fenton John Anthony Hort and Joseph B. Mayor, vol. 7 (New York: Garland, 1987). Frend also points out that Clement states he is also "wisdom, and knowledge and truth."

15. Frend, *The Rise of Christianity*, 370.

of God. Theophilus wrote an apology in three books directed to an educated pagan, *Autolycus*, c. 178–182. The latter asks how Christians see God. "Through creation," Theophilus replies. "Everything has been created from nothing, so that the majesty of God might be known and grasped by the mind through his works." God can be known through his handiworks and beneficence. "Thus God, who created all things by the Word and by Wisdom, can be known in His providence and in his works."[16] This relates to Paul's Epistle to the Romans, where "the invisible nature of God becomes visible in creation."

First, preparation is needed. The "spiritual eyes" must be opened. Theophilus writes that a person must first establish that man/woman has eyes to see and ears to hear; then it is the "eyes of the soul" being opened through which we may see God.

Faith in and fear of God must be established, to understand that God established his wisdom on earth, through his care. This may be experienced through a life of justice and purity, and only then, after death and resurrection, via "disposal of your corruptible nature, and clothed in incorruptibility, you will see God, in so far as you are worthy."[17] Theophilus does not mean that God is knowable only after death. "Disposal of your corruptible nature" means that we must be freed from the constraints of the human body, while still alive, no longer susceptible to the passions and sin, yet utilizing our body and its faculties to apprehend God.

Theophilus says knowing God through his works is hard through "carnal eyes," and inexpressible through words. Lossky explains:

> . . . as all is created from nothing, all there is, is what is created, or through His majesty, available to see God. If He is intelligent then God is known through prudence; power shows His energy; providence demonstrates His goodness; Father means that God is everything; fire conveys the notion of wrath.

---

16. Theophilus and Gustave Bardy, *Trois Livres à Autolycus*, Sources Chrétiennes (Paris: Cerf, 1948), Book 1, Chapters 1–7, p. 6.

17. Lossky, *The Vision of God*, 29.

This is an elaboration on specific tangible elements of creation as tied to attributes of the human being, and their analogies to God, as sensed and perceived through us. "Like the human soul which, while it remains invisible, makes itself known by the movements of the body which it animates, thus God, who created all things by the Word and by Wisdom, can be known in his providence and in his works."[18]

An eschatological framework of seeing and knowing God—after resurrection, predicated upon the requirement of existing in a perfected or incorruptible state upon death—may be found in the work of St. Irenaeus of Lyons (c. 175–185).[19] Such a state of purity, to Irenaeus, is the pinnacle of human endeavor. Knowledge of God is given to us through the Word (the Logos), a revelation from the Father through love, from which all things are created.

The Word becomes incarnated when humans are born. Before the Incarnation of Jesus Christ, humans were made in the image of God, but this could not be proven, because the Word—the One in whose image humans were made—was not visible. The Incarnation made the Word visible, and the image and likeness of God as human being demonstrated our own similarity to the Father. Irenaeus sees the Holy Spirit as the conduit for humans to acquire the likeness of God. It is through the Son and the Holy Spirit that we ascend to the life of God, he taught. God cannot be known through nature or creation; rather, he makes himself known by revealing himself via love, through our love for him and his love for us. Such knowledge does not come to us in our lifetime but after death.[20] To Irenaeus, there are three "visions" of God: first through the Holy Spirit, then through a "likeness" (similar to what Moses saw or experienced on Mt. Sinai), then through the Son, the Word made into flesh.

The concept of the light of God, made manifest through the uncreated Light, which shone from Jesus at the transfiguration on

---

18. Also a reference to Romans ("the invisible nature of God becomes visible in creation") and of Dionysius, who formed names from acts of providence and from Scripture. Ibid.

19. Cf. St. Irenaeus, *Against Heresies: False Gnosis Unmasked and Refuted*, written between 180 and 190.

20. Irenaeus, *Five Books of S. Irenaeus, Bishop of Lyons, against Heresies* (Oxford: J. Parker, 1872), IV 6, 3–6.

Mt. Tabor, is an important one in desert Christian and Byzantine theology. It is central to the doctrine of *hesychia* and would be the subject of the central dispute about the possibility of direct communion with God in the fourteenth-century Athonite controversies between St. Gregory Palamas and Barlaam. This "uncreated Light" is beyond creation; beyond the human senses, into the realm of the indescribable and invisible—the Father himself.

This vision of God in likeness is also a vision of life to come: the vision of Christ in his glory, the vision through which we are enabled to participate in the light of God, the Invisible. "To see the light," wrote St. Irenaeus, "is to be in the light and to participate in his life-giving splendor. Therefore, those who see God, participate in life."[21]

St. Irenaeus's vision of God is that of incorruptibility, as a source for eternal life and of all existence. Experiencing this vision of God entails participation. Through vision we participate in God, akin to light—to see it is to be in it. The invisible God is revealed by Christ transfigured by the light of the Father; the same light in which we may attain incorruptibility in a state of eternal life. To have a glimpse of light while on earth as human beings is possible only through the Incarnated Word, which is cast onto an eschatological plane, for the righteous.

It is important to realize that Irenaeus doesn't imagine any practical possibility of "seeing God." His theology's eschatological relevance to *hesychia*—or, more important, to the daily practice of *hesychasts*—is limited, as the revelation is yet to come. However, the possibility of participating fully in life with the possibility of seeing or communing with God in the hereafter is the hope of the life to come, essential for Christian faith.

THE VISION OR EXPERIENCE OF GOD IN SILENCE

The idea of the possibility of communion with God through contemplation began to develop from Hellenistic ideas, in Egypt, with the decline of eschatological notions and a shift toward a more soteriological and present-time modality of communion. Alexandria

---

21. Ibid., V 20, 1035.

was a locus of the shift, particularly in the writings of Clement and Origen and then of his disciple, St. Dionysius of Alexandria. The Alexandrian theological school does not believe that unity with God is possible only through the agency of resurrection or through a departure from the material world. Rather, we can unite with God in a material, corporeal existence, they believed, through use of knowledge. Here was a rejection of the idea of the future salvation after death in favor of a movement toward a method in this lifetime, open to all Christians, for attaining a new kind of perfection through devotion to God. The method to attain this perfection was through contemplation.

According to Festugière, Christians after third-century Alexandria also merged elements of pagan wisdom with the teachings of Jesus. He sees the origins of this school in the Alexandrian masters Clement and Origen, whom he calls the founders of "philosophical spirituality," that is, a kind of intellectual or superintellectual mystical practice. Festugière says, "Perfection is equated to contemplation, and to contemplate is to see God in an immediate vision." Festugière sees all subsequent Christian mysticism as a result of a symbiosis between Athens and Jerusalem. "The links in the chain are readily discerned. They are all teachers of contemplation: Evagrius, Gregory of Nyssa, Diadochus of Photice, the Pseudo-Dionysius in the East; Augustine and Gregory the Great in the West.[22]

The idea of the necessity of cleansing or purification took hold. Clement of Alexandria (c. 150–215), in his *Protrepikos* or *Exhortation to the Greeks*, finds that the Greek mysteries begin with purification. Christian confession, like Hellenic confession and pagan rituals, begins with the "lesser mysteries" and ascends to "great mysteries" of purification where we simply contemplate realities instead of acting on them, thereby learning from them.

The highest degree of contemplation of God, in Clement, is the end result of analysis and intellectual process. The process begins with *apatheia*, suppression of the body and its physical aspects for the purpose of liberating the mind's capacity to attain contemplation or knowledge. If we suppress the physical dimensions of mass and space—depth, size,

---

22. André-Jean Festugière, "Asceticism and Contemplation," in *The Child of Agrigento* (Paris, 1941), 131–46.

length—we can see ourselves as a single point in space. There, at that locus, we detect a "certain unity, an intellectual monad." If we then suppress all that is human in ourselves, both bodily and ethereal, what is left is the majesty of Christ. From there, we can then move on to experience knowledge of God, who "contains all." This is a particular kind of knowledge, "not of what is [as He is invisible] but what He is not."[23] This is an apophatic way, or a process of negation.[24]

The apophatic process helps us to know God, but not through our own devices. We know God when we put ourselves aside. Monks "negate" themselves, experiencing a kind of self-demise. They grieve for their sins and the sins of the world but at the same time receive the intimate and infinite joy of regeneration, forgiveness, and the spiritual joy of Christ's resurrection. The individual monk "dies" in order to live for God. He forgets himself in order to discover God. He surrenders and sacrifices worldly concerns and connections in order to attain true and real spiritual connection with God. This combination of renunciation, sorrow for one's sins, but joy in living for and with Christ is known as *harmolypi* (joyful sadness). This word expresses two emotions at once: sorrow and happiness. When one contemplates God through prayer and practice, and begins to deeply appreciate the many interventions and compassions of grace offered, the eyes are sometimes filled with tears, both of joy and of melancholy.

The contemplation of God takes us beyond the point of the One, beyond unity, into a realm that is beyond description. All experiences and ideas of this are by nature unformed, as God exists beyond form, type, difference, genus, or class. He is infinite, lacking any mass or dimension. No name can fully describe him: as Clement wrote, if we call him the One, the Good, Spirit, Being Itself, Father, God, Creator, Lord, we do so improperly; instead of pronouncing his name we are only using the most excellent names we can find among things that are known, in order to fix our wandering and disoriented thought.[25]

Hellenic philosophers also influenced Clement, particularly Plato who wrote in the *Timaeus*, "It is difficult to know God, it is impossible

---

23. *Stromateis* V, 11.

24. Reminiscent of Plotinus, in his sixth *Ennead*. Cf. Glossary.

25. *Stromateis* V, 12.

to express him." This statement makes it clear, to Clement at least, that Plato had read the Bible, borrowing the notion of the unnamable and unspeakable for God. He puts God into a region of ideas, the most difficult pinnacle of human reason to attain. For Clement, Plato learned from Moses' experience on Mt. Sinai that God contains all things in their entirety, but that we can only see him through a mirror, distantly, and not directly face-to-face. It is through our thoughts that we are able to see this dim light of divinity. Therefore, to Clement, Plato and Scripture are in accord.

Building on those practitioners who believed in and acted on the possibility of communing with God and in moving toward the specific history and methodology of *hesychia*, I see some emerging common patterns in the *hesychastic* tradition. Although Scripture often contradicts the possibility of communing with God, the desert ascetics believed it possible through likeness or image through the Logos, the Son of God, and later, the Holy Trinity, either in life or in the afterlife, through knowledge. They believed, too, that some form of purification is necessary.

The early desert *hesychasts* tell us that we can, indeed, see and know God. Clement explains that it's possible to become "likenesses" of God through the process of purification (as the Platonists and Stoics say) and by prioritizing knowledge, via the "transcendence of the Monad," the living Logos, the Son, Jesus Christ. Theophilus agrees that it is with the mind and intellect that we can know him, but in contrast to Clement, holds that it is through his provenance and works—creation.

Irenaeus takes an opposite stand: we cannot in this lifetime know God at all. It is only after death and resurrection that God may be realized in the afterlife.

Although it's impossible to summarize in one essay all of ancient Christian ascetic history on the subject of knowing God, it is evident that the theology, doctrine, and praxes of *hesychia* are based on the necessity of a hierarchical superiority of the mind (intellect) over the body in a Platonic sense, and that if God can be personally known or experienced, it is only by grace. A process of bodily and mental purification is necessary, sacrificing the pleasures and passions of the physical body and material world and the distractions of the mind, calling on the Holy Spirit through the Logos in the form of Jesus Christ to open the door for God's grace to enter.

The perfect place to put aside the physical demands of the body and the mental distractions inherent in civilized culture, for the purpose of being alone with God, was the desert.

ALONE WITH GOD IN THE DESERT

The word "desert" has its origins in Latin: *desertum*, "something left waste," from *deserere*, to "leave, forsake."[26] The Greeks have a word for desert, *eremos*, which means "abandonment." The word *hermit* is a derivation.

Yet the isolated, inhospitable desert holds attraction as a place to find deep spiritual wisdom, as also evidenced by the desert history of Judaism and Christianity. The Israelites wandered in the desert for forty years, fleeing perils and searching for God's word and salvation. Moses, while tending his father-in-law Jethro's flocks of sheep, climbed the desert boulders of Mt. Sinai to answer God shining down from the clouds, and in the nonconsuming flames of a burning bush.

Joseph and the Virgin Mary carrying the Christ-child, the Holy Family, fled to the deserts of Egypt to avoid King Herod's massacre of male children in Bethlehem (Matt. 2:16). Bishop Youannes comments,

> Egypt is the only land visited by our Lord Jesus Christ. The holy family came from Israel to Egypt and spent here more than three years and a half. . . . The holy family visited many, many places, and all of these places now became monasteries and ancient churches, so we consider Egypt as the holy land.[27]

John the Baptist preached of salvation in the arrival of the messiah, Jesus Christ, while teaching crowds in the desert. Christ began his testimony

26. *Compact Oxford English Dictionary of Current English*, ed. Catherine Soanes and Sara Hawker (New York: Oxford University Press, 2005).

27. HD Master Reel 22. Recorded January 19, 2007.

of total reliance on God while fighting demons in the desert for forty days and nights (Matt. 4:1–4):

> Then Jesus was led up by the Spirit into the wilderness to be tempted by the devil. He fasted for forty days and forty nights, and afterwards he was famished. The tempter came and said to him, "If you are the Son of God, command these stones to become loaves of bread." But he answered, "It is written, 'One does not live by bread alone, but by every word that comes from the mouth of God.'"[28]

God drew desperate people to the desert and appeared to them, assuring salvation from the limitations of human existence and worldly problems. The desert is a mystery: it is vast and void of life, because no human being can exist on sand and rock alone with little or no water, in the inhuman heat of day and the freezing cold of night. Yet the desert offers sacred visions and the presence of God, once one has surrendered their own understandings and experiences of worldly comforts and symbols of false gods, or has been brought to the edge of life and death.

How are we to find the desert in today's busy world?

John Chryssavgis writes, "The desert is an attraction beyond oneself; it is an invitation to transfiguration. It was neither a better way, nor an easier way. The desert elders were not out to prove a point: they were there to prove themselves."[29] Outwardly, it may appear that the early Christians experienced great suffering and trials in the desert; having to constantly worry about water and food, weather and harsh conditions. Externally, it may well have appeared that these people were dancing with insanity, wrestling with mental demons and casting away visions of the devil with constant prayer and meditation. However, some of the writings of the desert fathers and mothers paint a far more peaceful and joyous picture of desert life. The reasons they left civilization and their families behind were to find peace, joy,

28. NRSV. Oremus Bible Browser. http://bible.oremus.org/?passage=Matthew 4.1-4.

29. John Chryssavgis and Zosimas, *In the Heart of the Desert: The Spirituality of the Desert Fathers and Mothers: With a Translation of Abba Zosimas' Reflections*, Treasures of the World's Religions (Bloomington, IN: World Wisdom, 2003), 34.

and love with God, through the Holy Spirit and the Second Person Jesus Christ. They were in desperate need to free themselves from a multitude of useless thoughts (*logismoi*) and self-destructive actions dictated by uncontrolled desires. They wrestled with demons to win the victory of catharsis through grace. They endured suffering in order to discipline and cleanse their bodies and minds through total immersion into Christ. They surrendered their lives to the practices of stillness, watchfulness, and attentiveness in pure silence in order to see and hear the words and beauty of God himself. They looked for peace and found it in the complete isolation of the desert.

In the words of Bishop Youannes, General Bishop and General Secretary to His Holiness the late Pope Shenouda III, the former patriarch of the Coptic Church in Cairo:

> Of course, every person in the world needs the calmness of the desert, not only the monks or the nuns. . . . Because in the crowdedness of the world we don't see ourselves, and we don't see God. But when we [are] in a calmness, especially in the holy places, we begin to look to ourselves, to look to our shortages, to look to our defaults, to look to the deepness of our relation with God. To feel God, to hear God.[30]

Andrew Louth writes that the desert is not so much a place escape to; rather, it is a place to begin. The monks and nuns established relationships, with God and with their inner selves. These nomadic wanderers later grew to become communities of Christians: refining themselves and finding the revelation of God. The desert was a land of testing and preparation. It was the beginning and extension of a mission to know God and to serve God.[31]

To some practitioners, the desert was a place of retreat, stillness (eremia), or quiet (hesychia) where one could have the perfect condition for mental and physical withdrawal. To others, the desert was a place of life-and-death struggle, battling with the negative aspects of self and of sin. Louth says "a notable early example [of the

---

30. HD Master Reel 22. Recorded January 19, 2007.
31. Andrew Louth, *The Wilderness of God* (London: Darton, Longman & Todd, 1991), 1.

latter] is St. Antony . . . where the desert seems to be a noisy, clamorous place, worse than the world, not a place of quiet or stillness at all."[32]

32. Ibid., 2.

PART I

Development and Methodology of *Hesychia* through Stories of the Ancient Practitioners

---

1

The Great Hesychast Fathers and Mothers

In the deserts of Egypt, in the works of St. John Chrysostom, the Cappadocian Fathers and Mother, Evagrius Pontus, and in the *Apophthegmata Patrum (Sayings of the Desert Fathers)*, the word *hesychia* and its related *hesychazo* (withdrawal), and *anchoretism* (retreat) described a practice of desert- and cave-dwelling hermits who chose to seclude themselves for the purpose of quieting the body of its desires (*pathemata*) and the mind of its random distracting thoughts (*logismoi*).[1] Such practices enabled the ascetic to seek an empty internal place, away from worldly stimulus and problems, for the purpose of direct perception, experience, or vision of God.

Perched on the edge of the desert along the valley of the Nile, within sight of the settled land, the monks of second-century Egypt stood as a perpetual challenge to the situation of hunger and of total dependence on the distant marketplace that characterized the society of a starving and laborious Near East, according to Peter Brown. They, at least, had broken the dark cycle of hunger and avarice. In early writings we can glimpse the dreams of the early desert ascetics who knew what it was to starve. Wandering around giant stones, climbing bare-rock mountains, walking through scorching desert sand, constantly in search of wild herbs or infrequent springs that hosted oases—the desert dwellers caused themselves to enter a state of *adiaphoria*.[2] Robert T. Meyer writes, "The boundaries of man and desert, human and beast

---

1. G. W. H. Lampe, *A Patristic Greek Lexicon* (Oxford: Clarendon, 1961).

collapsed in chilling confusion. *Adiaphoria*, and not physical or sexual temptations, flamboyant and deeply humiliating though these might sometimes be, was the condition that the Desert Fathers observed most anxiously, and described most graphically, because they feared it most deeply in themselves.[3] What they sought was an ecstasy beyond physical sexuality, beyond the church or philosophy, into the realms of spiritual paradise.

The visible effects of *hesychia* inspired the rumor that its practitioners had attained the delights of paradise on earth. When a party of pilgrims compiled the *Historia Monachorum*, the Survey of the Monks of Egypt, around 400, the heroes they visited were men believed to have touched, and to have released for others, the huge and physical exuberance of Adam's paradise. The *Historia* relates that angels once arrived at the cell of Abba Apollonius and his companions, to bring them giant apples, great clusters of grapes, exotic fruits, and loaves of warm white bread. It was a foretaste of the sensual delights of paradise, granted to men who, by fasting, had chosen of their own free will to starve. This paradise was a land without the burning heat of day or the icy cold of the desert nights. Its gentle slopes were covered with rustling fruit trees, through which wafted nourishing, perfumed breezes. It lay just beyond the horizon of the cruel desert.[4] This was experiencing union with God, through *hesychia*.

In the *Sayings of the Fathers*, the memories of the great monks of Nitria and Scetis collected in the mid-fifth century, in the *Lausiac History* of Palladius, and in the lives and rulings of St. Pachomius and his successors, we can sense the huge weight that the myth of paradise-regained placed on the frail bodies of the ascetics.

2. Religious or theological indifference; indifferentism, latitudinarianism. *Oxford English Dictionary* online.

3. Palladius, *Palladius: The Lausiac History*, trans. Robert T. Meyer (Westminster, MD: Newman, 1965), 26–27.

4. *Historia Monachorum* 7: *Patrologia Latina* 21:416BC; *Apophthegmata Patrum*, Macarius 2:260C–261A; Bohairic Life of St. Pachomius 114, Veilleux, Pachomian Koinonia 1, 167–68. For the image/role of paradise in the Syriac world, see Ephraem of Nisibis, On Paradise 9.13 and 10.2–13, in R. Lavenant, trans., *Éphrem de Nisibe: Hymnes sur le Paradis*, 126, 135–40.

The ascetics imposed severe restraints on their bodies because they were convinced that they could sweep the body into a desperate venture that would result in divine reunion. For the average ascetics—ordinary, pious Christian men and women, squatting in cells within sight of the green fields of their villages or huddled together in the mud shelters of the Pachomian monasteries—the imagined transfiguration of the few great ascetics on earth spoke to them of the eventual transformation of their own bodies on the day of the Resurrection.[5]

His followers said of Abba Pambo, that just as Moses' face shone with the glory of the Lord, in the same way, the face of Abba Pambo shone like lightning, and he was like an emperor, seated on a throne. The same effect was to be seen in Abba Silvanos and in Abba Sisoes.[6] The faces of the enlightened reflected the state of ecstasy of mind, once cleansed of the demands of the body.

This positive condition, the result of communion between monk and God, was true for many other desert renunciants as well.

St. Antony

Although there were earlier monks and nuns living in desert caves and oases,[7] St. Antony (251–356) is considered by many to be the first Christian ascetic,[8] creating a Christian way of asceticism and monasticism, affecting the Orthodox Church for generations to come, and providing the essential ground from which the practice of *hesychia* as we know it sprang and was refined. Antony claimed his inspiration from Christ himself, the Word made flesh: Scripture was paramount in

5. Peter Robert Lamont Brown, *The Body and Society: Men, Women, and Sexual Renunciation in Early Christianity*, Lectures on the History of Religions (New York: Columbia University Press, 1988), 222.

6. Ward, *The Wisdom of the Desert Fathers: The Apophthegmata Patrum (the Anonymous Series)*, Pambo 12:372A.

7. Such as St. Paul, small communities of hermits centered around Alexandria and the Upper Nile region, and St. Pachomius, in the Thebaid.

8. Cf. Derwas J. Chitty, *The Desert a City: An Introduction to the Study of Egyptian and Palestinian Monasticism under the Christian Empire* (Crestwood, NY: St. Vladimir's Seminary Press, 1995), ch. 1.

his ascetic praxes and is central to St. Athanasius's telling of Antony's *Life.* The son of wealthy Alexandrian merchants, Antony one day was passing by a church and heard the priest instructing the parishioners about the apostles who gave up everything and followed the Savior (Matt. 4:20; 19:27), finding great peace and everlasting life. St. Antony was reminded of the community mentioned in Acts, where the followers of Christ sold everything and gave to the poor (Acts 4:34-5), and is said to have focused on the hope "laid up for them in heaven" (Col. 1:5; Eph. 1:18). Athanasius writes that Antony "obeys, very literally, the words of Christ":[9] he sold all his possessions, leaving his estate and all the family effects to his sister. This positive love for God and total dependence on Jesus Christ was St. Antony's armor, protecting him from the "demonic" urges of stray thought and temptations and the possibility of starvation and dehydration in the desert. The goal of his practice was to put himself aside, for God and for the charity and well-being of others.

Almost completely residing on the edge of life and death, St. Antony lived first in an abandoned tomb along the Nile in the Egyptian desert near Alexandria, then in a cave for forty-six years at the top of a craggy mountain near the Red Sea. When he emerged, his disciples found him vigorous and healthy, with a "cheerful countenance" reflecting "a glad heart."[10] He told an old monk, "Believe me. So great is the love in my heart for God that if my thoughts turn away from him for even a little, I weep like little children when their mother lays them down and hides herself a little while until she sees her children's love for her."[11]

Athanasius describes St. Antony as different from others not in height or size but rather in the makeup of his positive, happy character, a reflection of the purity of his soul.

9. Athanasius, *The Life of Antony*, trans. Tim Vivian et al., Cistercian Studies Series (Kalamazoo, MI: Cistercian Publications, 2003), 30.

10. Ibid., 201.

11. Tim Vivian and Rowan A. Greer, *Four Desert Fathers: Pambo, Evagrius, Macarius of Egypt, and Macarius of Alexandria; Coptic Texts Relating to the Lausiac History of Palladius*, St. Vladimir's Seminary Press "Popular Patristics" Series (Crestwood, NY: St. Vladimir's Seminary Press, 2004), 123–24.

> Because his soul was tranquil, Antony was also imperturbable on the outside; as a result, from the soul's joy he also had a joyful face and from the movements of his body one could sense and perceive the makeup of his soul. As it is written, "A glad heart makes the face bloom, but sorrow makes for a sad countenance."[12]

Living in desert tombs and caves meant having to subsist on very little water or food. St. Antony's sole purpose was to be with God. Any distraction—physical, psychological, demonic, external, and internal—was the same: a distraction. All he wanted was to love God. His way was to deny himself and his needs as completely as possible, leaving only God. While the material (outer) world was full of distractions and temptations, the inner world sought union with God through the absence of distraction, temptation, and stimulus.

St. Antony's direct spiritual experiences led him to teach tribes of disciples and to comfort them in God's grace during the fight "against the things of the world," and telling them of "the good things to come"[13] from God's love for humankind that has come to us in Christ. Through his instruction that God "did not withhold his own Son, but gave him up for all of us,"[14] he persuaded many to choose the monastic life. Monastic dwellings came into being in the mountains, and the desert was made a city by monks. Having left their homes, Athanasius relates, they registered themselves for citizenship in heaven.[15]

According to Derwas Chitty, St. Antony also possessed supernatural powers of healing the sick, fending off demons, and gracefully "comforting the sorrowful, reconciling those at variance, and urging all to put nothing in the world before the love of Christ."[16] Many followed his monastic model, and the desert became home for those inclined to a life of *hesychastic* solitude and contemplation.

---

12. Athanasius, *The Life of Antony*, 201.

13. Cf. Heb. 10:1.

14. Cf. Rom. 8:32.

15. Athanasius et al., *The Life of Antony*, 93. Cf. Luke 18:28; Phil. 3:20; and Heb. 12:23.

16. Chitty, *The Desert a City: An Introduction to the Study of Egyptian and Palestinian Monasticism under the Christian Empire*, 5.

A century later, Athanasius's *Life of Antony* made Antony famous for his ascetic practices throughout Christendom. Antony modeled and taught the possibility of individual communion with God through virtue.

> . . . virtue is not far from us,[17] nor does it stand outside us; it works within us, and the task is easy if only we want it to be. . . . The Lord has already said, "The kingdom of God is within you."[18] All virtue needs, then, is for us to will it, because it is within us and has its origins from us. Virtue comes into being because the soul[19] naturally possesses the rational faculty of understanding.[20]

St. Antony is saying that virtue and the kingdom of God are present internally, inside everyone, and accessible to anyone who wills it. His views indicate that he had been versed in Platonic philosophy, which subsumes philosophy into the realm of theology. All, according to St. Antony, may achieve the virtue of intellect that Plato portrayed as our highest pinnacle of life.

According to Peter Brown, the *Life of Antony* places St. Antony squarely in an "anti-intellectual" mode, signifying a shift of focus from those who would look to philosophy and philosophers to St. Antony himself, and by extension, to the man of God (specifically, a man of Christ). St. Antony is a holy man teaching that faith in Christ and ascetic practice is the new Christian way of education. "Paedagogus has exchanged his philosopher's mantle for the monk's habit."[21] Now, God could be available, internally, through virtue, to the uneducated monk. The *Life* not only brought a shift away from philosophy and from pagan and Hellenic culture to a Christian one. It offers the possibility of a new, internal, and personal—which is not

---

17. Cf. Luke 9:62.

18. Cf. Luke 17:21.

19. Greek: *to noeron*, from *nous*, "mind," the intellectual or rational faculty of human beings; in Platonic understanding, the *nous* was eternal.

20. Athanasius, *The Life of Antony*, 105–6.

21. Peter Brown, "The Saint as Exemplar in Late Antiquity," in *Saints and Virtues*, ed. John Stratton Hawley (Berkeley: University of California Press, 1987), 4.

to say *individual*—definition of virtue and theological knowledge—one that is of and centered in Christ. St. Antony, as portrayed in the *Life*, is bringing the reader to an internal life dependent not on culture and learning but on contemplation, ecstatic experience, and mystical wisdom. His methodology is counter to philosophy, a dominant force among the *Life*'s readers at the time. Tim Vivian notes, ". . . opposition, as we know, forces us to define our beliefs concretely and persuasively. For Athanasius, St. Antony's struggle against the philosophers shows what it means to be Christian."[22]

As far as methodology is concerned, St. Antony's way was to deny himself and his needs as completely as possible, leaving only God. The material (outer) world is full of distractions and temptations; the inner world must seek union with God through the absence of distraction, temptation, and stimulus.

In a well-known line, St. Antony speaks briefly to a visiting military commander about salvation, begging not to be kept away from his cave too long:

> Just as fish die if they stay too long on dry land, monks also grow feeble if they stay too long with you and loiter among you. Like fish hurrying to the sea, therefore, we too must hurry back to the mountain or we will stay too long and forget what is within.[23]

The requirement was to be alone with God on the mountain; to put aside one's sins, fighting a great demonic fight with one's internal demons, in favor of spiritual union. In speaking to Abba Pambo, St. Antony counseled,

> He who sits in the desert as a hesychast has escaped from three wars: hearing, speaking, seeing: but against one thing he must continually struggle—the warfare in his own heart.[24]

22. Athanasius, *The Life of Antony*, xlvi–xlvii.

23. Ibid., 239–41.

24. Ward, *The Wisdom of the Desert Fathers: The Apophthegmata Patrum (the Anonymous Series)*, Antony 4 and 11.

Ultimately, communion with God was found in silence and solitude, through grace. St. Antony knew this personally from his own experience: "Unless a man can say 'I alone and God are here,' he will not find the prayer of quiet."

St. Pachomius—Silence in Community

Another follower of St. Antony was a young eremitic monk, St. Pachomius (c. 292–348), who lived in *lavras*, or groups of cells, created by another follower named Marcarius for those unable to achieve the total seclusion demonstrated by St. Antony. St. Pachomius organized these individual dwellings into proto-monasteries, or communities, and is generally considered to be the founder of coenobitic, communal monasticism. Taken away from his family at the age of twenty by Roman armies and imprisoned as a traitor in a jail at Luxor, St. Pachomius was highly moved by the generosity of Christians bringing hot food and clothing to comfort the prisoners. When he asked them about their faith he was told they were men who followed the Son of God and hoped to emulate his kindness and charitable acts. St. Pachomius was then himself greatly inspired to also aid the suffering and sick.

Later St. Pachomius would often wander in the wilderness near his monasteries, collecting firewood, venturing through thorny brambles while praying; emulating the pain and suffering of Jesus Christ nailed to the cross. One day he came to a city, Tabennesis. While praying he heard a spiritual voice asking him to "stay and make a community of monks, a monastery."[25] A colleague, Palamon, helped him build cottages and huts, and later his brother John joined him.

According to Chitty, St. Pachomius's life was similar to St. Antony's, as his *hesychia* came in stages: first inner conflict with the *logismoi* or untamed, random thoughts, followed by a siege of demonic invasions, then growth, then perfect faith taking residence in the peace and calm of the heart. St. Pachomius had a direct vision of God in

---

25. Apostolos N. Athanassakis, *The Life of Pachomius: Vita Prima Graeca*, 7 vols., Society of Biblical Literature. Texts and Translations, Early Christian Literature Series, vol. 2 (Missoula, MT: Scholars Press for the Society of Biblical Literature, 1975), 11.

the form of an angel saying, "The will of God is to minister to the race of men, to reconcile them to Him."[26] What made St. Pachomius's teachings different from St. Antony's, according to Chitty, was that "Antony seeks to *be* perfect, Pachomius seeks to learn to do God's perfect *will*."[27]

The discipline in St. Pachomius's monastery was demanding. Everyone had to wear the same clothing: a brown habit, hood, tunic, goatskin mantle, and a girdle. There was a clear chain of command: monks in trades had supervisors who reported to the abbot, who was under the control of St. Pachomius himself. Prayers were said twelve times per day and twelve times a night. The Holy Eucharist was given twice a week.

Despite the strong hand of the monasteries' authorities and severe rules, they were extremely popular. When St. Pachomius passed, he left nine monasteries with hundreds of monks, and two nunneries, according to Frend. "Each Easter and on 13 August (Founder's Day) there would be a general assembly of the monks at the original house at Tabennisi. In Jerome's day (c. 390), nearly 50,000 monks would congregate to celebrate Easter."[28]

The wisdom of the desert sages spread east and west. The stillness and solitude of the desert were appealing, despite the vicissitudes.

THE CAPPADOCIANS: WE ARE GOD'S IMAGE AND LIKENESS

The Cappadocian Fathers and Mother—here represented by St. Gregory of Nyssa (c. 335–395), St. Basil the Great (c. 330–379), and St. Macrina (c. 325–380)[29]—advanced a theology centered on the idea of humankind, as we exist in creation, in the image and likeness of God. They followed the oracle of Delphi's "know thyself" (*gnothi*

---

26. Ibid., 23.

27. Chitty, *The Desert a City: An Introduction to the Study of Egyptian and Palestinian Monasticism under the Christian Empire*, 11.

28. W. H. C. Frend, *The Rise of Christianity* (Philadelphia: Fortress Press, 1984), 577.

29. Also called Macrina the Younger to differentiate her from her grandmother; or also Thecla, the name that was heard in a vision during her birth. Adding "mothers" to the Cappadocians will be no doubt controversial, but the author strongly sees the importance of this designation.

seaunton), yet believed it was difficult, if not impossible, to know the inner workings of humankind. St. Gregory of Nyssa taught that we should focus on the "ineffable mystery of God."[30] Yet he stated it was impossible to know God and that even understanding ourselves was unattainable.

St. Basil, while conceding that self-knowledge was the most difficult of the sciences, yet regarded knowledge of God through knowledge of the self, God's form and likeness, as positive and fruitful. Jaroslav Pelikan notes that St. Basil argued that knowledge of the self, "if carried out responsibly, was no less a 'light of theology,' and no less reliable a guide to the natural knowledge of God than was the knowledge of the world."[31] In a commentary on Ps. 138:14, on how "fearfully man had been fashioned," St. Basil wrote, "in observing myself, I have known thy infinite wisdom."[32]

The image of God in the human self was key to the Cappadocians, both as a possible way to know God and as the quality that elevates humankind above the earth it was created from, as it were, and the rest of the natural world. "Image of God" was synonymous with "likeness (*homoiosis*) of God" in the writings of St. Gregory of Nyssa.[33] St. Basil, in the *Liturgy of St. Basil*, writes, "Having shaped humanity by taking ground from the earth, O God, thou hast honored it with thine own image."[34] St. Gregory of Nyssa asked, "In what then does human greatness consist, according to the doctrine of the church . . . ?" (Pelikan adds, "and to the doctrines of natural theology?") St. Gregory responds: "Not in likeness to the created world, but in being in the image of the nature of the 'Creator.'"[35]

---

30. Saint Gregory of Nyssa, *La Création de l'Homme*, trans. J. Y. Guillaumin, Collection "Pères dans la Foi" (Paris: Desclée de Brouwer, 1982), 44:133.

31. Jaroslav Pelikan, *Christianity and Classical Culture: The Metamorphosis of Natural Theology in the Christian Encounter with Hellenism* (New Haven: Yale University Press, 1993), 122.

32. Basil, *In Hexaemeron*.

33. Saint Gregory of Nyssa, *Gregory of Nyssa's Treatise on the Inscriptions of the Psalms*, trans. Ronald E. Heine, Oxford Early Christian Studies (Oxford: Clarendon, 1995), 2.

34. Basil, *Liturgy of St. Basil*.

35. Gregory of Nyssa, *La Création de l'Homme*, 44:180.

Jaroslav Pelikan finds it essential to understand the position of the Cappadocians on the subject of knowledge of God via self-knowledge as articulated by St. Macrina, sister of St. Basil the Great and St. Gregory of Nyssa. Although there are no known primary texts of female ascetics from the fourth or fifth centuries, we do have a vivid account of her life and teachings through a biography, the *Life of St. Macrina*, penned by her brother, St. Gregory. He describes her as equal or superior to men, and depicts her as "sister, mother, teacher, and nun." He called her an "apostle," and a "Christian Socrates," stating that "in Christ there is no male or female, but in Him all are one." Carolyn L. Connor finds that "St. Macrina's voice is heard through Gregory's in an account that is gendered not in the sense of negative male bias, as is encountered in many medieval writings on women, but gendered by a male writer in support and praise of a woman."[36]

St. Macrina (325–380) was born to a wealthy family in Pontus in Asia Minor. When her fiancé died (she was twelve) she resolved to remain a virgin and take up the life of an ascetic. She made the family home at Annesi a monastery for both men and women, assuming the role of abbess. While some church officials, Jerome and Tertullian in particular, denigrated women citing scriptural authority, others found them to be equals, especially if involved in church activities. Patricia Cox Miller writes, "For wealthy aristocratic women in particular (about whom we know the most, thanks largely to the biographical literature that celebrated their achievements), an ascetic lifestyle offered possibilities for theological and scriptural education, scholarship, reflection, and friendships with male ascetics."[37] Wealthy women who adopted the ascetic lifestyle of *hesychia* could visit elders and spiritual masters, establish churches and monasteries, and held important jobs as teachers and advisors. Asceticism was encouraged, as well as celibacy, which had a reverse effect as women had more power and control over their lives than if they were married, and were perceived as threatening to church officials, according to Connor.[38]

---

36. Carolyn L. Connor, *Women of Byzantium* (New Haven: Yale University Press, 2004), 27.

37. Patricia Cox Miller, *Women in Early Christianity: Translations from Greek Texts* (Washington, DC: Catholic University of America Press, 2005), 192.

St. Gregory writes of his sister's *hesychia* and of the ascetic life in general,

> . . . for just as souls are free from their bodies by death and at the same time liberated from the cares of this life, so was their existence separated from these things, removed from all of life's vanity and fashioned in harmonious imitation of the life of angels. In them no anger, envy, hate, arrogance, nor any other such thing was seen; the desire for foolish things of no substance, for honor, glory, delusions of grandeur, the need to be superior to others, and all such things had been eradicated. Self-control was their pleasure, not to be known was their fame, their wealth was in possessing nothing and in shaking off all material surplus, like dust from the body; their work was none of the concerns of this life except in so far as it was a subordinate task. Their only care was for divine realities, and there was constant prayer and the unceasing singing of hymns, extended equally throughout the entire day and night so that this was both work and respite from work for them.[39]

St. Macrina taught that God himself as a subject is knowable, but how we commune with God is not. She articulated the difference between "that" and "how"—"the fact that 'that' [*hoti*] which was knowable, and the process 'how' [*pos*] which is not."[40] "How" is known only by the "truth itself," or God himself. "The 'that' of the image of God was sufficiently comprehensive as a concept for human nature to make it adequate as a designation even for the human nature in Christ."[41]

St. Macrina both defined and, according to tradition, exemplified a different understanding of the relationship between nature, God,

38. Connor, *Women of Byzantium*, 16.

39. Saint Gregory of Nyssa, *The Life of St. Macrina (Vita Sanctae Macrinae)* (Willits, CA: Eastern Orthodox Books, 1975), 11.

40. Gregory of Nyssa, *On the Soul and the Resurrection*, trans. Catherine Roth (Crestwood, NY: St. Vladimir's Seminary Press, 1993), 46:121.

41. Pelikan, *Christianity and Classical Culture: The Metamorphosis of Natural Theology in the Christian Encounter with Hellenism*, 123.

and our corporeal and noncorporeal dimensions. St. Gregory of Nyssa further described St. Macrina's life and that of other ascetics following her as a life "on the borderline between human and non-corporeal nature . . . but participating in the angelic and non-corporeal nature."[42] The body belongs to nature in a way that the soul does not, according to St. Macrina, because of the way we share the nature of the body with animals. However, arguing that there was no hierarchy of the soul over the body, against the position of the Neoplatonist Christians, and specifically Origen, St. Macrina insisted, "The point of commencement of existence . . . was one and the same for the body as for the soul."[43] In other words, both the body and soul are linked via nature at birth, yet at the same time the soul is noncorporeal and angelic, from God. She further said,

> The soul is an *ousia*[44] created, and living, and intellectual transmitting from itself to an organized and sentient body the power of living and of grasping objects of sense, as long as a natural constitution capable of this holds together.[45]

St. Macrina also wrote of "what her brother Gregory called 'the element of our soul in the likeness of God.'" This is the *Imago Dei*, the synthesis of the Platonic-Aristotelian-Stoic and Christian view of humanity, according to Emil Brunner, "which dominated the whole of the patristic period and the Christian Middle Ages, and has been and still is operative."[46]

St. Macrina's brother, St. Gregory of Nyssa, using the *apophatic* method of deduction on the "likeness of God," said in his *Orations on the Beatitudes*, in a famous commentary,

---

42. Gregory of Nyssa, *The Life of St. Macrina (Vita Sanctae Macrinae)*, 382.

43. Gregory of Nyssa, *On the Soul and the Resurrection*, 46:124–25.

44. Loosely, essence or substance.

45. Gregory of Nyssa, *On the Soul and the Resurrection*, 46:29.

46. Pelikan, *Christianity and Classical Culture: The Metamorphosis of Natural Theology in the Christian Encounter with Hellenism*, 123. Emil Brunner and Olive Wyon, *Man in Revolt: A Christian Anthropology* (Philadelphia: Westminster, 1947), 92–93.

When you hear that the divine majesty is exalted above the
heavens, that its glory is inexpressible, its beauty ineffable,
and its nature inaccessible, do not despair of ever beholding
what you desire. It is indeed within your reach; you have
within yourselves the standard by which to apprehend the
divine . . . [that is,] the likeness of [God's] own nature, as if
it were the form of a carving into wax.[47]

God is the form; we are the wax, the substrate material for God to
shape. We are nothing without God, empty and formless, subject to
melting and disintegration. The process of *hesychia*, and of prayer and
communion with God, is what forms us in his image and likeness.

In the fourth century, the Cappadocians forwarded the Platonic
triune notion of the Godhead in Trinitarian terms, as well as
combining "mystical and intellectual, intuition with reason" according
to Frend. St. Gregory of Nazianzus advanced the idea of God as
"worshipped in the Trinity and the Trinity is gathered into unity.
It is worshipped as a whole, and has royal power sharing a single
throne and a single glory . . . ,"[48] counteracting the Arian argument
of a singularly created human Christ, and the Apollinarian human
body but divine mind (Logos) concept of Christ. G. L. Prestige asserts
that St. Gregory of Nyssa originated the Christian idea of God as
"coinherence": the Trinity is of one essence, eternal and unchanging,
and all three aspects—Father, Son, and Holy Spirit—are all from the
Father.[49]

The Cappadocians, particularly St. Gregory of Nazianzus,
combined mystical notions and rituals with intellectual reason, and
placed the possibility of knowing God into a Trinitarian modality.

St. John Cassian: Systematization of *Hesychia*

Considered by Frend to have had an immense influence on
monasticism because of his categorization of *hesychasm* into stages of

---

47. Saint Gregory of Nazianzus, *St. Gregory of Nazianzus: Select Orations*, trans. Martha
Pollard Vinson (Washington, DC: Catholic University of America Press, 2003), Beatitude 6.
48. Ibid., Oration VI.22.
49. G. L. Prestige and F. L. Cross, *God in Patristic Thought* (London: SPCK, 1952), 268.

growth and development, St. John Cassian (c. 365–433) was a native of Dobrudja, in Rome's eastern Danube frontier. In his late twenties, around 392, he petitioned to become a monk at the monastery of the Nativity in Bethlehem. While visiting monks in Egypt, he became interested in a more solitary life. St. Cassian revered the Egyptian solitaries, but he believed that it took a special, highly prepared person to live in the desert. "It is perfect men who ought to go out into the desert,"[50] he stated in his *Institutes* (c. 426), St. Cassian's first work about the institutes and rules of monastic life, and a primer on how to avoid eight principal vices.

Later St. Cassian and his companion Garmanus would journey from Palestine and travel extensively in Egypt, where they learned about the monastic life from the great sages of the desert, the Christian abbots. Another book, *The Conferences* (c. 429), is a record of twenty-four dialogues with fifteen masters. For centuries, they have been considered a key work for monks, nuns, and scholars.

Early on, St. Cassian knew the distinction between desert and urban monasticism. If one is to become a monk, he taught, it was of vital importance to begin as a novice at a monastery that is more communally oriented, such as in a Pachomian community. His two earlier works prescribe what measures, step-by-step, were needed. Each precept was commented on by the masters. Novices were to attend services in the monasteries, which he considered temples of God. Owen Chadwick writes, "In fact this meant common worship in the five daily offices of Dawn (later Lauds), Terce, Sext, None and Vespers, to which was added a long vigil on Saturday from Vespers until the cock crow."[51]

St. Cassian taught that the monk, when not at services, should work. This effort consisted mostly of copying manuscripts, reserving agricultural work mainly for those more accomplished, or for anchorites—those who live in forests or islands near the monastery. Life was austere and difficult. Food was chiefly bread and vegetables. The

---

50. John Cassian and Boniface Ramsey, *John Cassian, the Institutes*, Ancient Christian Writers (New York: Newman, 2000), VIII. 16–19.

51. Owen Chadwick, *John Cassian*, 2nd ed. (London: Cambridge University Press, 1968), 77.

primary duty, thought St. Cassian, was for the monk to avoid the eight capital sins, moving steadily up the ladder toward virtue, to union with God through prayer and work.[52]

EVAGRIUS: GOD THROUGH PRAYER

Evagrius of Pontus (345–399) wrote the *Gnostic Centuries*, influenced by Plato and by Origen and later condemned by the Council of 533, yet still influential. Evagrius emphasized the importance of prayer and management of the bodily passions, creating the notion of "prayer of the mind," which is at the root of *hesychasm*.[53] Evagrius assigned such prayer the highest possible value. "Prayer is the proper activity of the mind," he wrote; ". . . an impassible state . . . the highest possible intellection."[54]

Evagrius described prayer in terms that equated it with divine union. Prayer offered an "equal state with Christ," like an "essential union" with God.[55] To Evagrius, to be in pure prayer is to be without any images or forms, in unity with the true God: totally, indescribably alive in the grace of the Holy Spirit. It is to be "in the Trinity itself," he said. In his *Chapters on Prayer*, Evagrius calls prayer a state where the soul is conscious of being in the divine presence.

> Prayer is the continual engagement of the spirit with its God. Consider, therefore, that state of soul that will be required to allow a spirit to strain after the Master without vacillation, and live directly and constantly in his presence.[56]

This state of grace in communion with and in love with God, to Evagrius, comes only after the monk prepares him- or herself properly

---

52. See Chapter 3, "The Journey of the Soul," ibid.

53. John Meyendorff, *Byzantine Theology: Historical Trends and Doctrinal Themes* (New York: Fordham University Press, 1974), 68.

54. Evagrius, *The Praktikos: Chapters on Prayer*, trans. John Eudes Bamberger, Cistercian Studies Series (Spencer, MA: Cistercian, 1970), 40:1272–76.

55. Ascribed to sixth-century monks, ibid.

56. Ibid., 3.

through mitigation of all human, bodily passions, sins of the flesh, or attachments of mind.

> The state of prayer is properly described as a habitual state of dispassion (*apatheia*). It catches up that spirit who loves wisdom in a rapture to the heights of intellective reality, that spirit which is truly spiritualised by the most intense love.[57]

Yet, Evagrius believed, one may arrive at this ecstasy only by grace; all else is but a prelude to the rapture and intense love of God. Even though we must make great efforts to prepare ourselves through *apatheia* and *hesychia*, all preparations are fruitless without the gift of grace.

Also known for systematizing ascetic practice, and his understanding and condensation of fourth-century Egyptian and Syrian ascetic practices and Biblical Scripture, and retransmitting them to generations of monks, Evagrius was a student of St. Gregory of Nazianzus and a follower of the theoretical and theological works of Origen after attending the Council of 381 at Constantinople.

Soon afterwards, he fled after an affair to the monastery of the Mount of Olives in the desert near Jerusalem. In 383 he took up residence at Nitria, a center of Egyptian ascetic activity, and then at Kellia.[58] An educated scholar, Evagrius was greatly influenced by the great nuns and monks, Melania the Elder, Rufinus, the two Macarii, and Palladius, and became the leader of intellectual monasticism. Building on the teachings of Origen that the human soul was once merged with God and had fallen to earth in sin, and on the nature of Jesus Christ (a denial of the physical resurrected body, contrary to Scripture), Evagrius posited that through ascetic effort the mind could be sharpened and clarified in preparation for the receipt of divine knowledge.[59]

---

57. Ibid., 52.

58. Known as "the innermost desert," Kellia ("the cells") was a fourth-century monastic community of single cells, formed about twelve miles south of Nitria. It was life in a coenobitic community in a semi-anchorite arrangement. Founded in 338 by St. Amun, it was discovered in 1964 by archaeologist Antoine Guillaumont.

Evagrius never spoke down to uneducated monks, reserving advanced teachings for gifted students. John A. McGuckin writes, "[Evagrius's] writings not only demonstrate a great stress on the path to imageless prayer that transcends thought, but also offered very practical levels of advice to ascetics on the controlling of psychological states, the taxonomy of virtues and vices, and the discernment of spirits."[60] Evagrius wrote of steps in the *Praktikos*, which consists of 100 chapters on asceticism, that the monk could take, in sequence, toward the goal of managing the body's influence, and understanding the will of God. Most of these steps are in short sentences, grouped in themes. The main practice that leads to spiritual knowledge is that of *hesychia*. *Hesychia* is achieved by practicing simplicity, frugality, and solitude—the benchmarks of *apatheia*.

Evagrius calls *hesychia* a "gift" from God, a gift of purity of heart and mind, in proportion to *apatheia* (passionlessness).[61] The gift is purity of heart, and the subsequent knowledge that ensues. Evagrius thought that the gifts of knowledge were in direct proportion to the alms given by the *hesychast* to the poor, and the efforts of his ascetic practices. He believed that in reaching perfect passionlessness, we would be "judged worthy of knowledge."[62]

According to Evagrius in the *Praktikos*, the way to perfect passionlessness is that monks should eat little and live in simplicity; avoid the distractions of sexuality, accumulation of wealth, and keeping servants (to avoid scandal or having to provide for them); and associate only with fellow brothers, avoiding connection with parents or relatives. This must be done in voluntary exile (*xeniteia*) in one's cell, avoiding the possible boredom by carrying out regular work and meditations. Regular fasting and practices of austerity and prayer are

59. This reflects a deep influence from Hellenic philosophy, specifically Plato's controlling of the bodily passions for the purpose of virtue; that knowledge was paramount and the ruler of the human being, and connected with God.

60. John Anthony McGuckin, *Standing in God's Holy Fire: The Byzantine Tradition* (London: Darton, Longman & Todd, 2001), 37–54.

61. Evagrius, *The Praktikos. Chapters on Prayer.*

62. Evagrius, *Sur les Pensées*, trans. Paul Géhin, Claire Guillaumont, and Antoine Guillaumont, Sources Chrétiennes (Paris: Cerf, 1998), 147 fn.

also necessary, in addition to a full liturgical life. Relations with members of the monastic community, the brothers, requires great humility and effort to never harbor resentments over what may come in the course of maintaining communal relationships.

Even though monks (and nuns) remove themselves to caves or monasteries to avoid the sensations and temptations of the actual world, Evagrius believed that memories of sensate-world experiences would still tempt and trouble the renunciant. These mental "demons" could be thoughts or fantasies from past experiences, thoughts of troubles or positive experiences; or they could be desires for praise or public recognition, leading to a swelling of pride or sparking vainglory. All, he thought, were due to psychological disorders or the work of demons.[63]

Once the *logismoi* disorders and demons had been purified and kept in abeyance, the presence of God could manifest. Spiritual ecstasy of the heart was the result. The idea of purification in turn brought a refocusing of the idea of baptism.

DIADOCHUS: CLEANSING THROUGH BAPTISM

Later in the fifth century, Diadochus, a bishop of Photice in Epirus and a participant at the Council of Chalcedon (451), wrote in his *Gnostic Chapters* that baptism, which he defined as a symbolic cleansing of the body and soul of impurities or sins by invocation of the name of Jesus Christ, was the foundation of the spiritual life. Grace was "hidden in the depth of our mind from the moment in which we were baptized, and gives purification both to the soul and to the body."[64] This wholeness of the human being was expressed through the "mysticism of the heart,"[65] as Diadochus locates the full human being in the heart:

---

63. Evagrius, *Evagrius of Pontus: The Greek Ascetic Corpus*, trans. Robert E. Sinkewicz, Oxford Early Christian Studies (Oxford: Oxford University Press, 2003), referring to *Praktikos* 7, 10, and 11, *Eulogios* 21, *Antirrhetikos* 4 (On Sadness).

64. Diadochus, *Oeuvres Spirituelles: Introduction, Texte Critique*, trans. Édouard des Places, Sources Chrétiennes; No. 5 Bis (Paris: Cerf, 1955), Ca77, 78, 135–36.

65. Ibid., 135–36.

> Grace hides its presence in the baptized, waiting for the
> initiative of the soul; but when the whole man turns toward
> the Lord, then grace reveals its presence to the heart through
> an ineffable experience. . . . And if man begins his progress
> by keeping the commandments and ceaselessly invoking the
> Lord Jesus, then the fire of holy grace penetrates even the
> external senses of the heart.[66]

Diadochus wrote of the importance of experiencing the Holy Spirit via
the heart, both internally (consciously) and externally, not limited to
the Evagrian concept intellectually. Symeon the New Theologian and
other Byzantine writers, according to Meyendorff, later appropriated
this personalization of Christianity.[67]

Diadochus, similar to Macarius, also sees recitation of the name
"Jesus" as the essential prayer, and central to monasticism. This is
a development after Evagrius, who taught prayer as an abstraction
and extension of general spiritual practice. This, to Meyendorff, is an
"essential orientation of spirituality toward the Person of the Incarnate
Logos, with a resurgence of the role played in Biblical theology by the
concept of the name of Jesus."[68]

Diadochus also wrote in the *Chapters* of the existence of both
God and Satan in the heart, but makes clear that Christians may
and actually must consciously experience the presence of Spirit in the
heart as well as in the mind. This is an important point: that the
whole person, both the heart and mind, must personally experience
God, unlike Evagrius's assertion that only the intellect can perceive
God. Diadochus's argument that one can have a direct and physical
experience of God would become foundational for later Byzantine
writers such as Symeon the New Theologian and Gregory Palamas.
Also, Diadochus forwards the method of constant repetition of the
name of "Jesus," a predisposition of faith oriented toward the Person of
the Incarnate Logos.

---

66. Ibid., Ca85, 144–45.
67. Cf. Meyendorff, *Byzantine Theology: Historical Trends and Doctrinal Themes*, 70.
68. Ibid.

St. John Climacus: God via the Jesus Prayer

In the sixth century, teachings of continued recitation of the name of Jesus were solidly established through the work of the Syrian-born St. John Climacus (c. 525–606).[69] A hermit for twenty years in a cave near Mt. Sinai, he was eventually persuaded by the monks at the monastery at Mt. Sinai to be their abbot at the age of seventy-five.

Climacus addressed the methodology of *hesychia* in greater detail. He explicitly defined three elements of the path to *hesychia* in practice: "Close the door of your cell physically, the door of your tongue to speech, and the inward door to the evil spirits." The *hesychast*'s direct experiences of inner peace and union with God, to Climacus, begin in external and internal recitation of the Jesus Prayer.[70]

Once in prayer, he observed, the practitioner will often lose the feeling of separation from God and may begin to quell his/her bodily passions and quiet undisciplined mental static, or *logismoi*. "*Hesychia* is to stand before God in unceasing worship. Let the remembrance of Jesus be united to your breathing, and then you will know the value of *hesychia*."[71]

Climacus demanded extreme discipline from his brethren, building on the work of Origen and Evagrius, specifying the keeping of passions in abeyance in his classic guide to asceticism, the *Scala* ("Climax") or *Ladder of Divine Ascent* (or *Ladder of Paradise*), one of the most widely read books in the Eastern Orthodox Church. St. Climacus wrote of thirty steps up a spiritual ladder in order to raise one's soul to God, who awaits the monk in the incarnate Jesus Christ at the top rung, at a door leading to heaven. Angels help along the climb, while demons attempt to shoot the monk down at any moment. Thirty steps correspond to the age of Jesus Christ when he was first baptized at the age of thirty, also the beginning of his ministry. In the *Ladder*, Climacus describes the importance of *apatheia* as the ultimate contemplative good in a human being, and the merits of constant

---

69. Also known as John Scholasticus and John Sinaites.

70. The Jesus Prayer: "Lord Jesus Christ, Son of God, have mercy on me a sinner," or just "Jesus."

71. John Climacus, *The Ladder of Divine Ascent*, Classics of the Contemplative Life (New York: Harper, 1959), Step 27.

prayer on the person and name of Christ involving the whole person, not just the mind. Meyendorff notes that St. John is using the "term *hesychia* ('silence,' 'quietude') and *hesychasts* designat(ing) quite specifically the eremitic, contemplative life of the solitary monk practicing the "Jesus Prayer."[72]

Later in the thirteenth and fourteenth centuries, St. John Climacus's methodology and terminology were widely appreciated, especially among later Byzantine *hesychasts*, practicing mental prayer tied to breathing. To Meyendorff, it is possible that the practice actually came directly from the monastery at Mt. Sinai, from Climacus himself,[73] although this point is controversial and difficult to certify. However, Climacus clearly did teach connection of mind and heart, toward deification of the whole person into the transfigured Christ. To "remember Jesus" was and is to monks an experience of divine presence, not just a symbol or simulacrum. This is done by evoking "Jesus" "in the heart," not just externally imagining, or thinking of the historical, or utilizing representational figures. To the monks it is about being united in God's presence via the sacraments,[74] beyond imagination.

His Eminence Archbishop Justinian Chira Maramureseanul of Baia Mare, Romania, portrays the Jesus Prayer and its cause or effect differently. He argues that the Jesus Prayer did not originate with St. John Climacus, but rather with the apostles themselves. "Because of the ascension of Christ to heaven, the apostles stayed alone and they started day and night to say this prayer—Jesus Christ, Son of God, have mercy. It was the only way to keep contact with the one who had ascended to heaven through thought, image, and sound."[75] The archbishop says on film about the Jesus Prayer,

> [w]hen the heart is pure, it starts elevating itself towards the mind, and it enlightens the mind, and it goes slowly down on the lips, and then the human being says, "Jesus Christ,

72. Meyendorff, *Byzantine Theology: Historical Trends and Doctrinal Themes*, 70.

73. Ibid., 70–71.

74. Called "Mysteries" by Eastern Christians.

75. Recorded January 23, 2007, Bucovina, Baia Mare, Romania. HD Master Reel 33.

Son of God, have mercy on me." So it is the opposite side by
which you proceed from the heart towards the mind toward
the lips.[76]

By the "opposite side," Archbishop Justinian goes against the Platonic
(and St. John Climacus's) hierarchy of mind in control of the body.[77]
Here, the purified heart is in control; the emotions and the affective
aspect of humanity inform the mind, illuminating the entire being,
infusing the whole person with prayer that floats up to the intellect.

St. Symeon the New Theologian: Visions of God

St. Symeon the New Theologian[78] (949–1022) made *hesychia* vivid in
his writing. He was known for communicating the reality of a direct
and total personal experience of God through prayer and spiritual
vision.

One evening during his prayers, Symeon experienced a powerful
vision of two radiant lights, one absorbed into the other.[79] John A.
McGuckin reports that St. Symeon interpreted the moment as a
"spiritual vision of how his spiritual father was interceding for him
before Christ at the very moment he was making his own prayers."[80]
Another vision happened where he experienced Christ directly in a
profoundly radiant light. As his visions were counter to St. Symeon's
own beliefs, he answered God, "For while hearing all this from Your
messengers, I presumed that this would occur in the age to come, after
the resurrection, and I did not know that it happened even now."[81]

76. Ibid.

77. In the case of St. Climacus, the apparent privileging of "mind" is almost certainly a
matter of "*nous*" being (poorly) translated as mind.

78. Given the title "New Theologian" after John the Evangelist and Gregory of Nazianzus,
both referred to as "Theologians."

79. Cf. J. A. McGuckin. "The Notion of Luminous Vision in 11th Century Byzantium:
Interpreting the Biblical and Theological Paradigms of St Symeon the New Theologian," in
M. Mullett, ed., *Work and Worship at the Theotokos Evergetis* (Belfast: Queen's University Press,
1997), 99–123.

80. McGuckin, *Standing in God's Holy Fire: The Byzantine Tradition*, 111.

81. Saint Symeon the New Theologian, *Catéchèses*, trans. Joseph Paramelle (Paris: Cerf,
1963), 66–92.

Later, in his *Catechetical Discourses, Theological and Ethical Discourses, Fifty-Eight Hymns,* and other writings, Symeon wrote of *hesychia* as a "personal communion with and a vision of God." This was not just a thought: St. Symeon meant a real and tangible physical meeting. This meeting with God is in the form of Jesus Christ. St. Symeon wrote, "Let us try, in this life, to see and contemplate Him. For if we are deemed worthy to see Him sensibly, we shall not see death; death will have no dominion over us."[82] The idea of a "sensible" vision, to Symeon, is without restriction to the confines of mind, heart, or soul. The word "sensibly" is of note here. St. Symeon is saying that the experience of God is a whole experience, involving not just the mind and intellect, but the whole sensory body and soul. This differs from Messalianism, and is not in opposition to the sacraments of the church, according to Meyendorff; rather, St. Symeon is trying to teach the brethren that the kingdom of God is "an attainable reality." This is not an experience to be received in the afterlife, but now, in this life. The experience of God is not restricted to mind or intellect as in Evagrius, but is a fully human one.[83]

"Through the Holy Spirit the resurrection of the body . . . [Christ] through his Holy Spirit grants, even now, the kingdom of heaven."[84] Beyond an eschatological communion and entrance into eternity after death, the kingdom of God's heaven is a real and present possibility.

This insistence that the kingdom of heaven is possible now made Symeon the New Theologian quite controversial. To his contemporary tenth- and eleventh-century monks, the practice of Christianity was about obedience and disciplined practices. St. Symeon deemed such a restrictive view heretical. His point was to become "like the holy Fathers . . . those who pretend that this is impossible . . . have not fallen into some particular heresy, but into all the heresies at once, since this one is worse than all in its impiety . . . whoever speaks in this way destroys all the divine scripture."[85]

82. Ibid., 421–24.

83. Meyendorff, *Byzantine Theology: Historical Trends and Doctrinal Themes,* 74.

84. Symeon the New Theologian, *Catéchèses,* 358–68.

85. Symeon the New Theologian, *Symeon the New Theologian: The Discourses,* Classics of Western Spirituality (New York: Paulist, 1980), Cat. 29, 166–90.

Yet, between 995 and 998 there were revolts by his monks because of his excessive demands on them to become saint-like. He was ultimately censured and relieved of his position as abbot due to "excessive veneration" of his father-confessor and for forwarding the Trinitarian Christology in direct experiential form in an actual presence.

John Meyendorff writes, "It is clear that Symeon stands for the basic understanding of Christianity as personal communion with, and vision of, God, a position which he shares with hesychasm and with the patristic tradition as a whole. . . . In the midst of tradition-minded Byzantine society, Symeon stands as a unique case of personal mysticism, but also as an important witness of the inevitable tension in Christianity between all forms of 'establishment' and the freedom of the Spirit."[86]

Even though Symeon held that we could consciously experience the grace of God in the here and now, Basil Krivocheine points out "he always had some reservations and emphasized that the fullness of knowledge belonged to the age to come."[87] Symeon taught that we should always struggle to commune with God now; he also said our struggles were "for the age to come." When he referred to the hereafter, he served his slight reservations about conscious experiential divinity: he must have carried some doubt.

Whether or not one has had conscious experiences of God, St. Symeon wrote, sins and passions serve us well nonetheless, and we are not freed of them if we have not had the divine experience. "If we have not put Him on in a conscious manner, like a coat, let us not think that we have been freed in the least from our disease and the passions that torment us . . . at least you are able to find yourself searching for Christ at the hour of death. At least you will be obedient to His friends. . . . You will find yourself serving Him through them. At least you fulfill the will of the servants of God and not your own—and the will of the servants of God is also His."[88]

86. Meyendorff, *Byzantine Theology: Historical Trends and Doctrinal Themes*, 74.

87. Basil Krivocheine, *In the Light of Christ: Saint Symeon, the New Theologian (949–1022), Life, Spirituality, Doctrine* (Crestwood, NY: St. Vladimir's Seminary Press, 1986), 165.

88. Ibid., no. 7, 353–55, 453–58.

Krivocheine sees that Symeon is talking about the obedience of monastic life and the necessity for surrender of one's own will, enabling us to serve God. Such service, however, is inferior to contemplation. Those who do not find God through asceticism, humility, and surrender have no excuse. Symeon wrote that when he found the light of God, his audience behaved as though they were "barking dogs." They would attack the seer; the one who gave witness of direct experience. "'Stop!' They would say, 'you deluded, arrogant man!' Who has become like the holy Fathers? Who has seen God or is able to see Him in the least? Who has received the Holy Spirit to such a degree that he was honored to see the Father and the Son? Stop, unless you want to be stoned."[89]

St. Symeon also got into violent conflict with a church metropolitan, Stephen of Nicomedia, after the official had canonized Symeon the Pious without official sanction. St. Symeon the New Theologian took the occasion to comment that there had not been hierarchical sanction; further, one should not be canonized without having experienced the vision of Christ. This was an example of "nothing but an intruder into the episcopate," proclaimed the New Theologian.[90]

St. Symeon intended to show a real and direct relationship between the kingdom of God, in the living Christ, and the living world, in the lives of human beings. He held this opinion not in opposition to the sacraments of the church but rather as a complement and realization of the institution and its purpose to spread the living gospel. While controversial to some of his contemporaries, the New Theologian was later canonized by the church and highly respected by generations of Eastern Orthodox Christians[91] as a great (or the greatest) mystic from the Middle Ages. Meyendorff notes, "By so doing, Byzantine Christianity has recognized that, in the Church,

---

89. Symeon the New Theologian, *Symeon the New Theologian: The Discourses*, #9, 364–75.

90. Symeon the New Theologian, *The Practical and Theological Chapters & the Three Theological Discourses*, Cat. Eth. 6, 406–54.

91. His designation as "theologian" also reflects his prominence (in the Eastern Church; only three sacred writers, St. John the Evangelist, St. Gregory Nazianzen, and St. Symeon are thus honored).

the Spirit alone is the ultimate criterion of truth and the only final authority."[92]

St. Gregory Palamas—Direct Knowledge of God for All Christians

Also stirring controversies about the direct experience of God later in the late thirteenth century and early fourteenth century was the Athonite monk, St. Gregory Palamas (1296–1359), who argued a doctrine of human knowledge of God along the lines of the New Theologian but clarified that we cannot by our own power or efforts know the "essence of God." His "essence" is forever unknowable, it is only by grace that his uncreated "energies" are revealed to us, or become spiritual experiences.

From early childhood, Palamas was interested in the church. Although born in Constantinople into a family of prominent officials of the court of Byzantine Emperor Andronicus II Paleologos, he neglected government opportunities and pursued monasticism. So enthralled, he convinced his brothers and sister and even his mother to join ascetic communities. He left the great city and around 1316 retreated to Mt. Athos, where he learned the ways of *hesychasm*. Continued Turkish invasions on the Holy Mountain caused him to move up to Thessalonica for a few years. He was made a priest in 1326, but he returned to Athos in 1331, where he lived at Vatopedi and then in a cave above Great Lavra.

In vogue at the time were teachings by an Italio-Byzantine monk, Barlaam of Calabria, who insisted that God was transcendent and that any human connection with him was impossible. This was counter to the growing school of *hesychasm* on Athos. In 1338 Palamas wrote a major tome titled *Triads in Defence of the Holy Hesychasts*, and his argument with Barlaam became intense and very public. The *Epistasia* or central clerical committee of Athos held a synod in 1340, approving Palamas's work, and issuing a statement called the "Hagioritic Tome," possibly under St. Palamas's direction. In this, Palamas's assertion that the experience of *hesychasm* is similar to what occurred on Mt.

92. Meyendorff, *Byzantine Theology: Historical Trends and Doctrinal Themes*, 75.

Tabor—that the uncreated light emanating from Christ at his transfiguration[93] was an eschatological light of the kingdom of God to come—was upheld.

St. Palamas articulated his theology of direct communication with God in three theories: 1) Knowledge of God, upon baptism and with participation in the life of the Body of Christ in the Eucharist, is given to all Christians. The human through both the intellect and a "spiritual sense," a presence neither physical nor intellectual, knows God. This is based on Christ assuming the whole of humanity, in body, mind, and soul, thereby deifying us. Thus, in the *hesychast* method of prayer, according to St. Palamas, we are participating in both human and divine life. 2) God is inaccessible in essence and may only be perceived through his "energies," or that which is "created" and material. Only the three hypostases are "good by essence." Humans can only become God by "grace," or by "energy."[94] 3) There is a strong difference between "energies" and "essence." God is not found in philosophical structures; he is a living God, both transcendent and immanent. Through God's energies, in the material, created world, we can realize him. In Christ it is the Logos that is hypostasized, becoming human through the energies. These are given to creatures as gifts of grace from God.

Palamas's distillation of *hesychast* theology, *One Hundred and Fifty Chapters*, posited that monastic *hesychast* practices were "the whole purpose of Christian life." The goal was to purify the heart and enter so deeply into the contemplation of God that one might be chosen as an elect disciple and, like the three apostles, be called up to see the divine

---

93. ". . . and his face shone like the sun, and his garments became white as snow and behold, there appeared to them Moses and Elijah, talking with him. And Peter said to Jesus, 'Lord, it is well that we are here; if you wish I will make three booths here, one for you and one for Moses and one for Elijah.' He was still speaking when lo, a bright cloud overshadowed them, and a voice from the cloud said, 'This is my Beloved Son, with whom I am well pleased; listen to him.' When the disciples heard this, they fell on their faces with awe. But Jesus came and touched them, saying, 'Rise, and have no fear.' And when they lifted up their eyes, they saw no one but Jesus only. And as they were coming down the mountain, Jesus commanded them, 'Tell no one the vision, until the Son of Man is raised from the dead'" (Matt. 17:1-92; see also Mark 9:1-9; Luke 9:28-36; 2 Peter 1:16-18).

94. The Cappadocians affirmed this inaccessibility, against Eunomius and Origen.

light that shone around Christ on Tabor. This light, the uncreated light of God, is a reflected light that is visible to created beings, humans, versus the actual light of God which is not possible to see, as we are not of the same nature as God. It is energy of God, not the essence.

> This shining light and deifying energy of God, which deifies all who participate in it, constitutes divine grace, but is not the nature of God as such. By this I do not mean that the divine nature is separated from those who have grace . . . since the Divine Nature is present everywhere. What I mean is that it is unapproachable, for no created thing can participate in the divine nature as such . . .[95]

The Calabrian Italo-Greek philosopher, Barlaam, argued in opposition to Palamas that God was unknowable other than through indirect means: from Scripture or unique revelation. He attacked *hesychasm* as a kind of "Messalian materialism,"[96] or a psychosomatic[97] method of prayer.

In response to Palamas's first theory, Barlaam countered that this experience was not intellectual, and was "an obstacle to a true encounter." Barlaam further objected to *hesychastic* prayer as too physical, sarcastically calling practitioners "navel gazers."

After years of debate, the Council of 1341 condemned Barlaam for attacking the Athonite monks. Palamas's testament of a living God through grace was endorsed in 1347, 1351, and posthumously in 1368, when he was canonized.

---

95. Saint Gregory Palamas, *The Triads (Défense des Saints Hésychastes)*, trans. Nicholas Gendle, Classics of Western Spirituality (New York: Paulist, 1983), 3.

96. The Messalians (from the Syriac for "praying group") were a group of mystics, beginning in the fourth century, who were condemned as heretics. They were accused of abandoning the Scriptures and advocating a direct, material connection with God. Ultimately both the Eastern and Western churches denounced their practices.

97. Physical and mental; an experience that is at first illusory or imagined but becomes physically felt due to the power of the mind's effect on the body.

St. Gregory of Sinai: Systematizing Prayer and Direct Communion with God

St. Gregory of Sinai (1255–1346), a monk tonsured at St. Catherine's Monastery at Mt. Sinai, later fled the invasions of the Turks to Mt. Athos and was a contemporary of St. Gregory Palamas. Both are known for teachings on the technical method of *hesychasm*, expanding on Evagrius and Climacus, involving the connection of breathing to recitation of the Jesus prayer, as well as a specific bodily position of bowed head and gazing at the abdomen while in a totally isolated locale.

The Philokalia contains five of St. Gregory of Sinai's works. The following instruction is an example of his different view of the attainment of *hesychastic* prayer:

> Noetic prayer is an activity initiated by the cleansing power of the Spirit and the mystical rites celebrated by the intellect. Similarly, stillness is initiated by attentive waiting upon God, its intermediate stage is characterized by illuminative power and contemplation, and its final goal is ecstasy and the enraptured flight of the intellect towards God.[98]

This instruction is different because it is both the Holy Spirit that is doing the cleansing of the *nous*,[99] as in St. Symeon, and the efforts of the ascetic him- or herself. Here, Gregory of Sinai labels contemplation as an intermediate step. Unlike Plato or Evagrius, St. Gregory of Sinai differentiates the intellect from God: the *nous*, or the ability to perceive

---

98. Nicodemus and Makarios, *The Philokalia: The Complete Text*, v4.237.

99. Generally, *nous* is mind or intellect in the West; soul, or that which perceives God, in the East. *Nous* may take several meanings: the soul or spiritual aspects of a man (as in St. Isaac the Syrian), as well as the heart, or essence of the soul (cf. *Philokalia*, vol. II, 109, 73). It may be portrayed as what is behind, or the core of the soul (St. Didochos, ibid., 79 & 88). It is sometimes referred to as the "eye of the soul" (*The Orthodox Faith*, St. John of Damascus, FC vol. 37, 236). The *nous*, or energy of the soul, might be called "a power of the soul" (*On the Holy Spirit*, St. Gregory Palamas, 2, 9) "consisting of thoughts and conceptual images" (*On the Hesychasts*, St. Gregory Palamas, 410, 3), described by Elder Joseph the Hesychast, *Monastic Wisdom: The Letters of Elder Joseph the Hesychast* (Florence, AZ: Saint Antony's Greek Orthodox Monastery, 1999), 404.

God, is different from the mind or intellect—a Greek perspective to this day.

St. Gregory of Sinai remained isolated in a *skete*[100] on Mt. Athos, sending his disciple Isidore away to return to the world. St. Gregory Palamas also left the *skete* and ultimately became a prominent archbishop.

THE PHILOKALIA: A COLLECTION OF HESYCHAST FATHERS

From eleven centuries of monks at Mt. Athos, and from *hesychasts* in the desert lands of Egypt, Roman Palestine, and Syria, came a collection of words and instructions about the experience of God and the monastic practice of *hesychia* called *The Philokalia*, a Greek word meaning "the love of the beautiful, the exalted, the excellent . . ."[101] Collected by St. Nikodemos of the Holy Mountain and St. Makarios of Corinth, first published in Greek in 1782, the collection of theory and praxes has been published in many languages. Editors Palmer, Sherrard, and Ware published the most recent edition in English in 1979. The work is mainly an instruction manual for monks, although it may be used selectively by laypersons. Some Orthodox consider it to be a secondary guide to spiritual practice along the lines of the *Apophthegmata Patrum* and the *Ladder of Divine Ascent*, the primary being the Holy Scriptures.[102] In *The Philokalia*, the texts are focused on the purification of the intellect, so that one may be "illumined and made perfect." Describing the great *hesychast* saints, the English editors write,

> They describe the conditions most effective for learning what their authors call the art of arts and the science of sciences, a learning which is not a matter of information or agility of mind but of a radical change of will and heart leading man towards the highest possibilities open to him,

---

100. A small hut or primitive building separated from larger communities of monks, often in a forest or mountainside.

101. Nicodemus and Makarios, *The Philokalia: The Complete Text*, 13.

102. "Philokalia,"

shaping and nourishing the unseen part of his being, and helping him to spiritual fulfillment and union with God.[103]

The conditions in *The Philokalia* described as *hesychia* are silence and tranquility, and also drawing from the original Greek root denoting being seated, still, and fixed in one place and time. In order to attain this condition, the prerequisite is total adherence to morality as directed by Scripture and the Commandments, followed by continued recitation of the Jesus prayer, regular partaking of the Holy Eucharist, and solitude.

The editors and translators make a strong point that some contemporary historians mistakenly argue that these practices are the result of a movement in the thirteenth and fourteenth centuries centered at Mt. Athos. This is incorrect, as they assert the practices are indicative of a whole spiritual tradition from the beginning of Christianity itself. This is evidenced by the facts that the Jesus prayer was "integral to the texts included," which were written before the ninth century and are desert wisdom from the time and place where asceticism originated, as we shall see below.

---

103. Nicodemus and Makarios, *The Philokalia: The Complete Text*, 13–14.

2

An Analysis and Comparison of Ancient Practitioners and Methodology

The concept of putting oneself into a location and state of silence and stillness for the purpose of communion with God, behind the practice of *hesychia*, has not changed much since it began in the early second century. However, the lifestyles, methodologies, and methods of transmission have changed.

ISOLATION OR COMMUNAL LIFE?

The earliest ascetics left civilization and retreated to the desert in isolation. Whether in secluded caves or in community with other *hesychasts*, ascetic life consisted mostly of prayer and a hunt for water and minimal amounts of food. Benedicta Ward says, "The ideal was not sub-human, but super-human, the angelic life; but this was to be interpreted in the most practical and common-sense way."[1] This did include renunciation of life's luxuries, but it did not mean complete self-denial, such as fasting for long periods, or extra-harsh obeisances. "The monks went without sleep because they were watching for the Lord; they did not speak because they were listening to God; they fasted because they were fed by the Word of God. It was the end that

---

1. Benedicta Ward, *The Wisdom of the Desert Fathers: The Apophthegmata Patrum (the Anonymous Series)*, Fairacres Publication (Oxford: SLG, 1975), xiv.

mattered, the ascetic practices were only a means."[2] The life of a nun or monk was about continual determination, but not intense struggle. The earliest ascetics in Upper Egypt eventually formed communities, but the opposite was the case for St. Antony, who remained eremitic, a hermit who lived by himself, apart from any towns or communities.

Asceticism for St. Anthony and others like him was never the end, only the means. Ward explains, "The aim of the monk's life was not asceticism, but God. It was important to follow Christ's example, to help the poor and sick, and to love the neighbor."

St. Athanasius calls St. Antony "a physician given by God to Egypt."[3] He portrays him as consoling, blessing, listening to confessions, and giving advice to both his disciples and visitors. Ware finds his charitable care for others similar to Palladius's account of how Eulogius ministered to a "cripple,"[4] and to the ministry to a diseased pilgrim by the Russian Zosima, whom Dostoyevsky saw in the Optima Hermitage and on whom he modeled his monastic priest character by the same name in *The Brothers Karamazov*.[5]

It is important, starting from this early stage, to understand the statement that the early eremites were making in withdrawing from the world. St. Antony's flight away from people was not world-denying, but world-affirming in his aid for others. His teachings were biblical and consisted of direct obedience to the teachings of Christ, essentially to love God and perfectly follow a path of righteousness, primarily through prayer and aiding others.

Scripture or Liturgy?

St. Antony puts great emphasis on Scripture. Counseling that all of life must be true to the gospel, St. Antony believed that the Bible was

2. Ibid., xvi.

3. Athanasius, *The Life of Antony*, trans. Tim Vivian, Apostolos N. Athanassakis, John Serapion, Rowan A. Greer, and Benedicta Ward, Cistercian Studies Series (Kalamazoo, MI: Cistercian Publications, 2003), 87.

4. Palladius, *Palladius: The Lausiac History*, trans. Robert T. Meyer (Westminster, MD: Newman, 1965).

5. Fyodor Dostoyevsky, "The Brothers Karamazov," NetLibrary, 1976.

the only true instruction needed for the life of the *hesychast*. When someone asked St. Antony what rules are the most important to follow, he replied, "Wherever you go, have God always before your eyes; in whatever you do or say, have an example from the Holy Scriptures; and whatever the place in which you dwell, do not be quick to move elsewhere. Keep these three things and you will live."[6]

The church did not retain St. Antony's almost exclusive emphasis on Scripture as a guide to the *hesychastic* life. Bishop Ware finds that contemporary Orthodox Church teachings encourage but do not mandate reading of Scripture by monks. Often attending Eucharist suffices. "[T]he Liturgical services which they are attending, especially at Great Feasts and during Lent, are very lengthy and contain frequent repetitions of key [scriptural] texts and images. All this is sufficient to feed the spiritual imagination of the worshipper, so that he has no need in addition to rethink and develop the message of the church services in a daily period of formal meditation."[7]

We find alternative paths to *hesychia* as far back as the early centuries of the church. Others found different ways of peace than retreating to solitude in the desert. St. Pachomius did not find peace in the solitary life guided by an occasional visit to a spiritual master. Instead, believing that human beings were created to be social, he started his own different type of monastery more focused on community. St. Pachomius found isolation and personal perfection to be almost impossible, and even counterproductive. He believed in discipline and putting aside one's self, but taught that it was best to practice *hesychia* in community.

Of the Pachomian communities Jerome wrote, "Brethren of the same trades are lodged together in one house under one superior. For example, weavers are together; mat-makers are reckoned as one household—each trade is under the rule of its own superior. And week by week, an account of their work is rendered to the abbot [*Patrem*] of the monastery."[8]

6. St. Antony 3, in Benedicta Ward, *The Sayings of the Desert Fathers: The Alphabetical Collection* (London: Mowbrays, 1975), 2.

7. Kallistos Ware, *The Orthodox Way*, rev. ed. (Crestwood, NY: St. Vladimir's Seminary Press, 1998), 111.

The Cappadocians represented a third variation in the early practice and context of *hesychia*. They mixed asceticism and social life in community, but unlike St. Antony and St. Pachomius, were highly educated intellectuals and placed great emphases on education. St. Basil the Great, along with his brother, St. Gregory of Nyssa, and friend, St. Gregory of Nazianzus, are remembered as "the Cappadocian Fathers," referring not just to where they were born but to their profound and widespread influence on the history of Greek-speaking churches and monasticism. Frend, referring to the Cappadocians, wrote that "Eastern monasticism, a Trinitarian orthodoxy that combined piety and intellectual rigor, with a sense of zestful movement in theology, laid the foundations of what became Byzantine Christianity—all due in part to these three extraordinarily gifted and dynamic men."[9] Taking the best elements of a life of singular practices of *hesychia* and mixing them with learned social life without the intense rigors of anchoritism, the Cappadocian Fathers made orthodoxy highly appealing for many people. This is perhaps what Frend means by "zestful" theology: a more God-filled life in relationship with philosophy and communal life.

8. Jerome, *Regular S. Pachomii translatio Latina* praefatio VI. In J. P. Migne, *Patrologia Latina the Full Text Database* (Ann Arbor, MI: ProQuest Information and Learning Company, 1996), http://www.columbia.edu/cgi-bin/cul/resolve?ANC0798.

9. W. H. C. Frend, The Rise of Christianity (Philadelphia: Fortress Press, 1984), 630.

3

Evolution of Monastic Life

St. Basil gleaned this balanced societal and intellectual life of *hesychia* visiting bishoprics in the East, "so that the contemplative life might not be cut off from society, nor the active life be uninfluenced by contemplation, according to St. Gregory of Nazianzus."[1] The hermit life was replaced by a more Christian-Platonist fellowship, notes Frend.[2] St. Basil's ideas about education of both mind and soul were rooted in Hellenic philosophy. Pericles, Plato, and Socrates espoused a tradition of holistic education that St. Basil carried forward into Christian catechism and instruction in ascetic worship. Classic philosophy was concerned not only with creation of civilizations and government systems, but also with care of the soul.

THE RULE AS BASIS FOR MONASTIC PRACTICE

St. Basil's *Rules* (in long and short form) were designed to aid the individual monk and also support the monastery. His instructions in the form of questions and answers (thus the original name *Asketikon*) are of significance, as they are the basis for most monastic practices still in use today by Eastern and Greek Orthodox, as well as some Greek Catholic communities.

---

1. Gregory of Nazianzus, *Oration* XLIII (Panegyric in Honor of Basil), in J. P. Migne, *Patrologia Graeca: Patrologiae Cursus Completus, Seu Bibliotheca Universalis, Integra, Uniformis, Commoda, Oeconomica Omnium Ss Patrum, Doctorum Scriptorumque Ecclesiasticorum*, Graeca (Paris, Parisiorum: http://phoenix.reltech.org/Ebind/docs/Migne/Migne.html, 1857), 36.

2. W. H. C. Frend, *The Rise of Christianity* (Philadelphia: Fortress Press, 1984), 630.

St. Basil developed his *Rules* to encompass not only personal salvation but also the maintenance of family-like relationships and giving service to others. The goal of the spiritual seeker should be the common monastic life. St. Basil's monasteries were therefore small and closely knit, sharing common attire, property, work, and prayer. There were to be six prayer services per day, and two at night. Eucharist was celebrated four times a week. Frend detects the influence of Pachomian communities that St. Basil visited, although St. Basil added more dimensions to his, such as a more organized system of communal worship.

DESERT OR CIVILIZATION?

Frend concludes that St. Basil's monasticism "came as near as any movement within the early church to a Christianity that aimed at changing society and transforming organized religion into a social as well as an individual creed."[3] What St. Basil contributed to *hesychia* was that it didn't have to be practiced in seclusion. Focus on God through prayer and ascetic practices within a group was a valid pathway to individual salvation and liberation from materialism. This could be done in desert or urban isolation.

In fact, St. Basil even condemned anchoritism, according to Irénée Hausherr, "in the name of the human social character." This differentiates him from the other Cappadocians.[4] *Hesychia* was important to St. Basil and his monasteries; in his *Rules* he strongly advocated putting oneself aside in favor of Christ. Renunciation followed the gospel, and he insisted on strict obedience to it and the community's abbot. Hausherr points out that St. Basil "understood the Gospel [rules] of renunciation, here and elsewhere . . . members of a community 'must demand strict observance of them from one another . . .' it is not surprising that most of the 313 *Short Rules* present the details of this total renunciation almost exclusively, and the ways of having the cenobites practice it."[5]

---

3. Ibid., 631.

4. Irénée Hausherr, *Spiritual Direction in the Ancient Christian East*, Cistercian Studies Series (Kalamazoo, MI: Cistercian Publications, 1989), 166.

St. Basil's sister, St. Macrina, also subscribed to the combination of urban life with asceticism. The difference of philosophy between St. Macrina and her brothers, Sts. Basil and Gregory, was that she believed God could be known through an image or "likeness," the *Imago Dei*, but that our souls, while born to and linked with nature, are ultimately noncorporeal. Establishing the proper setting for the practice of both *hesychia* and the liturgy within monastic life, St. Macrina taught of the possibility of the revelation of God's grace in likeness. She was one of the first to establish monasteries for women, who had been earlier excluded from asceticism. In her monastery the ordinary concerns of women, the childrearing and care for the husband and home, were alleviated. Nuns could concentrate their life entirely on prayer and worship and could travel to meet with spiritual masters and scholars, and be free of all worldly ties. This was not the case for other women.

Regarding a life of *hesychia* and focus on the likeness of God, her brother St. Gregory Nyssa wrote in his biography of his sister,

> Their only care was for divine realities . . . this was both work and respite from work for them. . . . For to have freed nature from human passions was a feat beyond human strength, while to appear in body, to be encompassed by bodily shape and to live with the organs of sense, was thereby to possess a nature inferior to that of the angelic and the incorporeal.[6]

Like St. Macrina's ascetic life of mitigation of bodily distraction in favor of the divine, St. John Cassian took the life and education of a coenobitic monk and further systematized it, focusing on the importance of the monk finding and maintaining *apatheia* (dispassion and management of bodily desires and impulses), which he translated from the Greek as "purity of heart." This is a major shift from the centrality of the human intellect in his predecessors.

5. Ibid., 70.

6. Gregory of Nyssa, *The Life of St. Macrina (Vita Sanctae Macrinae)*, in Patricia Cox Miller, *Women in Early Christianity: Translations from Greek Texts* (Washington, DC: Catholic University of America Press, 2005), 197.

St. John Cassian is considered to have brought Eastern desert monasticism to the West: he left Egypt for Constantinople and became closely allied with St. John Chrysostom, who ordained him a deacon and entrusted him with his church. He later established two monasteries near Marseilles, and it was there that he wrote his *Institutes* and *Conferences* pertaining to the rules of monastic life and the avoidance of the Eight Principal Vices for the benefit of his *hesychast* disciples, and to further Egyptian asceticism. After St. Chrysostom's exile, he went with an envoy to Rome to argue his mentor's case with Pope Innocent I, where he was ordained a priest.

St. Cassian later became controversial because of his teachings that salvation was the result of human effort and free will, instead of God's grace. It could be argued that this was in reaction to Augustinian thought, bringing him closer to the views of Pelagius, but that is a vast subject astray from the matter of *hesychia*.

Here we move from a consideration of different models of *hesychia* in the context of monastic life, from isolation and societal rejection to community life and service to a closer examination of methodology via examination of a doctrine of *hesychastic* prayer by Evagrius of Pontus.

Using a Neoplatonist concept of the intellect as divine and in hierarchical control of the body, and building on the metaphysical teachings of Origen, Evagrius Pontus developed a doctrine of *hesychia* mostly centered on prayer. He wrote that prayer is an "ascent of the mind to God."

Evagrius believed that a permanent "prayer of the mind" or "mental" prayer is the central point of eremitic or *hesychastic* life, far more important than community or group worship. Meyendorff explains that Evagrius saw prayer "as natural to the human mind . . . in prayer, man becomes truly himself by reestablishing the right and natural relationship with God."[7]

Evagrius sought to define prayer more precisely than his predecessors and to understand its effect on the one who prays. Ultimate prayer, to Evagrius, was beyond words, according to William

---

7. Gregory Palamas, *The Triads (Défense des Saints Hésychastes)*, trans. Nicholas Gendle, Classics of Western Spirituality (New York: Paulist, 1983), 2–3.

Harmless. *Hesychastic* prayer involves the Greek concept of *nous*, or the intuitive and spiritual aspect of humanity. To be in continual prayer is to awaken and exercise the *nous*. Harmless notes that Evagrius does not consider this state as *ekstasis* (ecstasy) or to "stand outside oneself." Rather, it brings us to a point of *katastasis*, a unity with one's true state of being.

Evagrius taught that we do not have any command to stay up all night in vigils or for fasting, but pointed to the injunction of Paul in 1 Thess. 5:17 to "pray without ceasing." Evagrius also specified that prayer contain no images; it should be "formless."

> When you pray, do not try to represent the divine in yourself, do not let any specific form be imprinted on your mind. Instead approach the Immaterial immaterially, and then you will understand.[8]

PRAYER AS COMPLETE TRANSCENDENCE

Harmless believes that to Evagrius, God is beyond the limits of materiality, "beyond shape, color or time, and to pray before any image, even a mental image is idolatrous. Thus the one praying must seek complete transcendence."[9] This meant transcendence of all material, especially oneself. This is an important concept in Evagrius. Naming mind as "natural" yet beyond all materiality[10] was something that would bring him great controversy because of his apparent circumnavigation of the Second Person of the Trinity. Evagrius was condemned by the Ecumenical Council of 553 because of his Origenistic metaphysical beliefs, yet his method of prayer has continued to be important in Byzantium and in Orthodoxy in general. Later, in Eastern Christian Orthodox practices, notes Meyendorff, the prayers of Evagrius took on a Christocentric spirituality.

---

8. Evagrius, "De Oratione" 66, in William Harmless, *Desert Christians: An Introduction to the Literature of Early Monasticism* (Oxford: Oxford University Press, 2004), 79.

9. Ibid., 351.

10. Indicating Evagrius's subscription to the metaphysics of Origen.

The "mind" ceased to be opposed to matter, because Christian monasticism fully accepted the implications of the Incarnation. Thus, the "mental prayer," addressed by Evagrius to the Deity, which he understood in a Neoplatonic and spiritualized sense, became the "prayer of Jesus."[11]

We begin to see the repeated Name of Jesus invocation in subsequent Eastern Orthodox ascetic practitioners and masters for years to come. Evagrius's theology and doctrines of prayer are of crucial and pivotal relevance to *hesychia*: the continued recitation of the Jesus Prayer as the core method and doctrine.

The writings of an unknown monk using the pseudonym of Macarius came into prominence. Ps. Macarius's writings also were centered on the name of Christ but radically different from the Neoplatonic intellectual teachings of Evagrius. In opposition to Evagrius's assertion that the center of prayer is in the mind, Ps. Macarius argued that the locus of human awareness was in the heart. Important *hesychasts*, especially St. Gregory Palamas, would later make this notion paramount. Ps. Macarius stated,

> The heart is master and king of the whole bodily organism, and when grace takes possession of the pasture-land of the heart, it rules over all its members and all its thoughts; for it is in the heart that the mind dwells, and there dwell all the soul's thoughts; it finds all its goods in the heart. That is why grace penetrates all the members of the body.[12]

Ps. Macarius is teaching us that through the grace of Christ, present as the Incarnated Father in our heart, our prayer can transform our entire being, body and soul.

Evagrius thought humans to be primarily intellect and saw Christianity as a process of "dematerialization" into a realm of more

---

11. Gregory Palamas, *The Triads (Défense des Saints Hésychastes)*, 2–3.

12. Pseudo Macarius, *Die 50 Geistlichen Homilien des Makarios*, Patristische Texte und Studien (Berlin: De Gruyter, 1964), Hom. 15, 20, p. 139.

mind and *nous* and less bodily influences. Ps. Macarius understood people to be a psychosomatic whole, destined for "deification." He opposed the Platonic, Origenian, and Evagrian philosophy that mind and soul are separated from the body. To him, it was impossible for the mind to be removed from the body, either in life or ultimate destiny. It was Ps. Macarius who forwarded a spirituality of baptism and the Eucharist as methods of unification with Christ and of "deification" of the entire human, including body, mind, and soul. "The fire which lives inside, in the heart, appears then (on the first day) openly and realizes the resurrection of the bodies."[13] Ps. Macarius is saying that after the moment or first day of baptism or acceptance of the Eucharist, the heart opens and becomes deified, thereby realizing the immortality of the entire human being through Christ.

So it follows that the Evagrius prayer of the mind, in Ps. Macarius, is transformed into the "prayer of the heart." The locus of a human being's psychosomatic state is the heart, the "table where the grace of God engraves the laws of the Spirit."[14] The locus of the heart can also have a negative context: the heart can be a place where "the prince of evil and his angels find refuge."[15] So Ps. Macarius sees the heart as a battleground between God and the Devil, and monks at the center of the fight between good and evil.

We will see the importance of the distinction of the practices of *hesychia* and of prayer as centered in either mind or heart, and especially in the reunion of heart and mind through the next centuries of Orthodox *hesychia* and monasticism into the present.

The Christocentric essence of the repetition of the Jesus Prayer, employing either the mind or heart, in either a Neoplatonic or somatic sense, reverberated through *hesychia* for centuries, continued and expanded by monks such as St. Diadochus of Photice (fifth century) and St. John Climacus (sixth century). Both remained true to Christian biblical and incarnation themes in the context of Hellenist philosophy.[16] St. Diadochus of Photice linked baptism and the

---

13. Pseudo Macarius, *The Fifty Spiritual Homilies; and the Great Letter*, trans. George A. Maloney, Classics of Western Spirituality (New York: Paulist, 1992), 11, 1.

14. Ibid., 15, 20.

15. Ibid., 11, 11.

invocation of the name of Jesus to generate a personal experience of God. St. John Climacus developed both a specific repetitive prayer and a systematic method of ascension to God.

What was new with St. John Climacus at the monastery of Mt. Sinai was the constant repetition of the Jesus Prayer, focused on the experience of *hesychia* at a constant and almost somatic level, "Lord Jesus Christ, Son of God, have mercy" (or the Greek, *kyrie eleison*) in short-sentence form, also tied to breathing. St. Climacus also taught, "*Hesychia* is to worship God unceasingly and to wait on him. . . . The Hesychast is one who says, 'I sleep, but my heart is awake.'"[17] This constant repetition, like breathing, becomes automatic, involving the entire person consciously and unconsciously. It is an intellectual practice that goes deep into the psyche and transforms human beings into a state of being beyond the intellect or emotions.

In general the word *hesychia* stands for an internal state of soul, according to Ware. "It denotes the attitude of one who stands in his heart before God." This connection with God occurs day and night, in unceasing prayer, for the rest of his or her life. This is what silence and stillness mean to the *hesychast*.[18] St. John Climacus provides a classic description of what it means inwardly to practice *hesychia*: "A solitary is he who strives to confine his incorporeal being within his bodily house, paradoxical as this is."[19] This is a difficult concept to explain because in many ways we are all trying to confine something incorporeal within the confines of the body, if one believes in the concept of the soul as divine. However, for St. John Climacus, the continual recitation of the Jesus Prayer offered a new possibility for replacement of the limited human self with God; a new selfless focus. Meyendorff describes: "Faithful prayer eventually empties the heart of all concerns

16. Cf. *The Philokalia*, a primary source for Greek *hesychast* traditional writings.

17. Quoting Song of Songs 5:2. John Climacus, *The Ladder of Divine Ascent*, trans. Colm Luibhéid and Norman Russell, Classics of Western Spirituality (New York: Paulist, 1982), No. 27, pp. 263, 69–70.

18. Thomas Merton, *Merton and Hesychasm: The Prayer of the Heart*, ed. Bernadette Dieker and Jonathan Montaldo, The Fons Vitae Thomas Merton Series (Louisville: Fons Vitae, 2003), 20.

19. Climacus, *The Ladder of Divine Ascent*, Step 27, No. 6, p. 237.

and even all thoughts, so that it may be filled by communion with the One. Once the child has asked for all she wants, once she turns all her desires over to her father, her mind is prepared to contemplate him in silent awe. In the early *hesychast* tradition, one simply calls on Jesus' presence to enter silently into one's heart, continually."[20] This is a simple yet profound aspect of *hesychia*, the petition for the grace of God through continued and focused contemplation and prayer.

This notion of an incorporeal being in a corporate form would reverberate through the ages from Byzantium and into present time through the teachings of the Athonite St. Gregory Palamas. In different words than his predecessors, St. Palamas made a distinction between "essence" and "energy."

HYPOSTATIC UNION

The main point of what St. Palamas taught that is so important to *hesychia* is the central importance of the "One Who Is"[21] becoming man. Beyond the God-man relationship in mediated form argued by Ps. Dionysius the Aereopagite; beyond the intellect of Evagrius or the metaphysics of Origen; God, to St. Palamas, was immediately present.

> Did He not deign to make His dwelling in man . . . to appear to him and speak to him without intermediary, so that man should be not only pious, but sanctified and purified in advance in soul and body by keeping the divine commandments, and so be transformed into a vehicle worthy to receive the all-powerful Spirit?[22]

It is possible, St. Gregory believes, to experience direct communion with Christ, or "in Christ" (or energy), preserving our full human nature, yet directly experiencing God's transcendent essence, always "above" the limited human conception of the experience. We can experience God's energies, but not his essence. Our communion is not,

---

20. See John Meyendorff, *St. Gregory Palamas and Orthodox Spirituality* (Crestwood, NY: St. Vladimir's Seminary Press, 1998), 20–40.

21. A reference to God's answer to Moses on Mt. Sinai.

22. Gregory Palamas, *The Triads (Défense des Saints Hésychastes)*, 21.

according to St. Gregory, with "created grace," but with God himself. This is what the experience of the "uncreated energies" means. This stems from the Christological doctrine of "hypostatic union."[23]

Hypostatic union in other words refers to the "personal" incarnation of the *Logos*, the second person of the Trinity. God becomes human in his body through deification, becoming penetrated with divine life, or "energy." This is what is happening in the Eucharistic bread and wine, as communing with God "in Christ," as St. Palamas describes:

> Since the Son of God, in his incomparable love for man, did not only unite His divine Hypostasis with our nature, by clothing Himself in a living body and a soul gifted with intelligence . . . but also united Himself . . . with the human hypostases themselves, in mingling himself with each of the faithful by communion with his Holy Body, and since he becomes one single body with us (cf. Eph. 3:6).[24]

Participation in the Eucharist, the central point of the liturgy, is thus of vital importance to the *hesychast.* The human union with God, in spiritual and material form, is the result of God's grace; *hesychia* is a method of readiness and preparation.

The methodology of continual prayer, acknowledgment of God in Christ and the confession of sin are essential as well. The method of prayer, *hesychasm*, linked to the inhalation and exhalation, which is practiced today in Orthodox monasteries throughout the world, began on Mt. Athos with St. Palamas.

> . . . certain masters recommend them to control the movement inwards and outwards of the breath, and to hold it back a little; in this way, they will also be able to control the mind together with the breath—this, at any rate, until such time as they have made progress, with the aid of God,

---

23. "Hypostatic" is a Christian technical term denoting the union of the divine and human in the person of Christ. It became official at the Council of Chalcedon.

24. Gregory Palamas, *The Triads (Défense des Saints Hésychastes)*, 19.

have restrained the intellect from becoming distracted by what surrounds it, have purified it and truly become capable of leading it to a "unified recollection." One can state that this recollection is a spontaneous effect of the attention of the mind, for the to-and-fro movement of the breath becomes quieted during intensive reflection, especially with those who maintain inner quiet in body and soul.

Such men, in effect, practise a spiritual Sabbath, and, as far as is possible, cease from all personal activity. They strip the cognitive powers of the soul of every changing, mobile and diversified operation, of all sense perceptions and, in general, of all corporal activity that is under our control; as to acts which are not entirely under our control, like breathing, these they restrain as far as possible.

This Palamite method of reciting the Jesus Prayer linked to the breath, focusing the mind on the purified body, is a union of mind and heart, intellect and *nous*, a summation by St. Palamas of centuries of *hesychastic* doctrine and practice. In the words of St. Palamas,

you will be able to present yourself with boldness to "Him who searches the veins and the heart"; and that indeed without His scrutinizing you, for you will have scrutinized yourself. Paul tells us, "If we judge ourselves, we will not be judged." You will then have the blessed experience of David and you will address yourself to God, saying, "The shadows are no longer darkness thanks to you, and the night will be for me as clear as the day, for it is you who have taken possession of my reins." David says in effect, "Not only have you made the passionate part of my soul entirely yours, but if there is a spark of desire in my body, it has returned to its source, and has thereby become elevated and united to you."

The *hesychast* has offered body, mind, and soul to God. Linkage has been made between God and human, in silence and stillness, in admission of sin with petition for grace. What we see in St. Palamas is that the composite of soul and mind (in the Neoplatonic sense) has been managed, allowing the *nous*, the spiritual pinnacle, to develop in stillness and silence.

The Alexandrian/Egyptian desert tradition of eremitic practice, the Syrian tradition of contemplation on the soul, and the method of prayer focused on the unification of mind and heart have come together on Mt. Athos in the fourteenth century with St. Palamas, and to a lesser extent with his contemporary, St. Gregory of Sinai. Now with the centrality of the Jesus Prayer begins the link between *hesychia* and the Athonite link to *hesychasm*. The *Hesychast Tradition* had begun.

With the methods put forward by St. Gregory Palamas and St. Gregory of Sinai built upon those *hesychasts* before them, it was possible to see the uncreated light of God through the created human being. This conscious awareness of God, present in our humanity in vision, intellect, and emotion, inspired Byzantium and the collection of stories and admonitions known as *The Philokalia* around the eighteenth century. It is still the primary influence on Eastern and Greek monastic practice, as we shall see in the next section on contemporary practitioners and their methods.

We shall now see the ancient words and practices of both the desert and Athonite masters alive and well in the caves and monasteries where they began, in the breath, bodies, and minds of contemporary *hesychasts*.

4

Hesychia Provides Peace and Connection to God for Individuals

This section will highlight contemporary methods of peace and connection to God through practices of *hesychia*; how practitioners, selected *hesychasts*, and church officials in the areas of Egypt, Mt. Sinai, Greece, and Romania teach and use it; and what it means to them. I have picked specific *hesychasts* in historically significant locations representing a range of doctrine, spiritual experience, and hierarchical positions within each monastery they represent.[1]

ON THE EXPERIENCE OF PEACE THROUGH *HESYCHIA*

As the practice of *hesychia* began in the Egyptian desert, this is where we begin our discussion of peace through *hesychasm*. Asceticism is alive and well in monasteries in Egypt. Coptic Bishop Youannes says that there has been a steady increase of monks and nuns over the last twenty years, many with advanced degrees and established careers upon arrival and acceptance into the monasteries:

> During the days of jurisdiction of His Holiness Pope Shenouda III, there was a flourishing of the monastic life. Thirty-five years ago [when the pope received his responsibilities, there were only seven monasteries]. Nowadays in Egypt we have about twenty-four monasteries

---

1. Which also coincide with the ethnographic field video documentary, a part of this book.

and about ten nunneries. . . . We have in Egypt more than one thousand five hundred monks.[2]

The increase in *hesychasts* reflects a general increase in Coptic Christianity, largely due to His Holiness the late Pope Shenouda III's ecumenical work and dedication to religious unity. He was the first Coptic pope to meet with the pope of the Roman Catholic Church in over 1500 years. He assisted the expansion of Coptic churches in America, Africa, and other countries, and made sure that the Copts were full members of the World Council of Churches, the Middle East Council of Churches, the All-African Council of Churches, the National Council of Churches in Christ in the USA, the Canadian Council of Churches, and the Australian Council of Churches. In May 2000, he established the Office of Ecumenical Affairs in the Archdiocese of North America.[3]

Father Lazarus, the *starets* of the Coptic monastery of St. Antony on the Egyptian Red Sea, spoke on-camera about his first meeting with His Holiness Pope Shenouda III. He had been a professor in Australia and an atheist in his youth. Eventually, he joined the Serbian Orthodox Church but claimed he had never felt a sense of peace and never had the chance "to be alone with God." He wanted to come to Egypt and become a monk, as he knew monasticism had begun there, and thought it was necessary to come to the desert to feel God. He said, "When I met the Coptic pope, I said to him, 'I would like to come to Egypt to feel the love of God in the desert.' [The pope] looked at me and said, 'If you have the love of God in your heart, you can be happy anywhere.' But I said, 'But that's what I don't have in my heart here. I want to find it in the desert.'"[4] The Coptic pope then welcomed him to Egypt.

To Father Lazarus, finding peace requires being solitary. Living in a cave on the mountain above the monastery not far from St. Antony's cave, Father Lazarus also feels the peaceful presence of this first desert

---

2. HD Master Reel 22. Recorded January 19, 2007.

3. Pope Shenouda III of Alexandria.

4. Recorded January 18, 2007. HD Master Reels 19–20.

father who started *hesychia.* He knows that to feel the peace of God, one must have silence in order to listen.

Father Lazarus is now the spiritual master of the monastery, father to over 150 monks. However, most of his time is not spent in community; weeks or months can go by for him in total silence and seclusion at home in his cave.

Peace to him is internal. He explains that it is possible to go to a beautiful garden or forest, and to breathe slowly and be very peaceful, but this is temporal. The best kind of peace is that of the mind. He can be alone in his cave for weeks or a month, but his mind may be very active or be somewhere else. What Father Lazarus recommends is prayer to become internally silent, on an automatic basis, in order to find true peace, with the mind stilled and thoughts void of *logismoi*—the distractions of the material world.

Between Mount Sinai and Mt. Horeb on the Sinai peninsula rests the sixth-century St. Catherine's Monastery and Church of the Transfiguration, on the other side of the Red Sea from St. Antony's Monastery in Egypt. Here Moses is said to have seen God's backside on the mountaintop and in the nonconsuming flames of the burning bush (Exod. 3:2). This is among the oldest continuously working monasteries in the world.

The *igoumen* (abbot) of St. Catherine's Monastery, His Eminence Archbishop Damianos (Samartzis), said that this region in the Sinai was the best place to practice *hesychia* as it is an exceptionally quiet and peaceful place. It is far from anything else: no cities or villages, buildings, or domiciles of any kind.

His Eminence Archbishop Damianos disclaims that he is a *hesychast*, considering himself more an administrator who makes *hesychia* possible for his monks, but admits that he is certainly an ascetic. He identifies himself as "an intellectual monk, who prays the Jesus Prayer, but often misses church," according to his "sloth," he explains. I find this to be the archbishop's humility in evidence.

He is extremely hardworking and is frequently traveling to other churches and monasteries under his charge in the Archdiocese of Sinai[5]

5. His Beatitude Archbishop Damianos is the Superior of all Greek Orthodox monasteries and churches in Egypt, the Pharan and Raitho. Though consecrated by the Patriarch of

and is often unavailable to celebrate the daily liturgy, yet is often present for Sunday Eucharist at the Church of the Transfiguration, at St. Catherine's.

His Eminence Archbishop Damianos uses the Holy Trinity to find peace through God in Jesus Christ. "Without Christ, the second person of the Holy Trinity, we cannot get to the Father, and without the Holy Spirit, which will reveal Christ to us, who will in turn give us all of the Trinity, we cannot reach the Father." That is, we must utilize the Holy Trinity to approach God, as our minds are incapable of direct communion. "No human mind can ever fully comprehend the *Theia Ousia* (Divine Substance)."[6] This is why the monk must think of, and repeat, the Holy Name of Jesus at all times.

His Eminence Archbishop Damianos teaches that "[w]e must not stop talking about God, as long as we don't make any mistakes and fall into philosophical *diatiposeis* [ontological appraisals, of our own imagination]." The archbishop cautions that in our practice of *hesychia*, we must put ourselves aside and never think our lives are the result of our own doing or being. He teaches that it is only Jesus Christ through the Holy Spirit who can forgive our sins; only Christ, the anointed one of God, who is able to give God's mercy and God's grace.

Building on both the Christian and Hellenist traditions of the hierarchy of mind over body and the necessity of mitigating bodily and selfish desires, His Eminence Archbishop Damianos says, "Christ asks of us to reach perfection, helping us by endowing us with logic and all the gifts (*charismata*) as well as the body, which is a necessary obstacle in order to work the virtues and move forward towards illumination [*theosis*]." Here, *apatheia* is the purification process. Virtue guides us to God. It is not only beliefs that aid the monk in experiencing peace and communion with God, the practices of *hesychia* and prayer are necessary as well. When our virtues are purified and our human nature

---

Jerusalem, he is not his subject. The Church of Sinai is the smallest Eastern Orthodox Church, and one of the oldest in the world still in operation. Cf. *The Blackwell Dictionary of Eastern Christianity*, ed. Kenneth Parry and John R. Hinnells (Oxford: Blackwell, 1999), "Sinai," p. 451.

6. Recorded January 16, 2007, Mt. Sinai. HD Master Reel 8/9.

set aside, then we are freed to be open and clear. The light of Christ may then shine forth.

We must be careful in action and in practice, His Eminence Archbishop Damianos cautions. "There is always the fear that we get confused, when there are clearly two natures joined together mysteriously, supernaturally, without change. But sometimes the Divine Nature acts more; other times it's the human nature of Christ. Just like in the crucifixion, the human nature of Christ suffers, not the Divine."[7] Unlike in Christ, our human nature is prone to sin and suffering; *hesychasm* is the way to let the Divine shine forth, offering us the grace of peace, enlightenment, and deification. It's vital to remember that we are more than our human nature, and not to be deceived into thinking that we are just our human nature.

His Eminence Archbishop Damianos also spoke at length about the importance of the Holy Trinity, and about the ability of Jesus Christ to assist us in purification of the soul in order to experience internal peace and salvation.

> Christ Himself says in the Gospel, "I am the Way," and also, "I am the peace which supersedes every *nous*." This peace is an internal peace, which is incomprehensible to the limited human *nous*, because people cannot understand how great this peace is, which is associated with joy. In the monastic as well as the Christian [worldly] life we also have the spiritual struggle or, in other words, the personal struggle in order to achieve the cleansing of the soul. Despite the various external methods of struggle to achieve this *catharsis* [cleansing] there is a great peace, tranquility and joy in the soul. This joy is a very important thing, and in order to help us remember, we use a term in monasticism called *harmolypi* [joyful sorrow]. Joy for Jesus Christ and sorrow for our sins.[8]

In looking back on centuries of *hesychia* and at the same time looking at the present practice, it is important for *hesychasts* and those seeking

7. Ibid.
8. Recorded Tuesday, January 16, 2007. Reel HD 8.

spiritual peace to remember that ancient writers frequently refer to positive, joyful experiences of God, but at the same time there is a kind of sorrow, or *penthos*. Sorrow may not be the most accurate translation; rather, as Archbishop Damianos puts it, *harmolypi* is a feeling of simultaneous joy and regret when faced with the awe of an encounter with God, as mentioned earlier.

In order to truly practice *hesychia* and to find genuine spiritual peace and connection with God, the ancients wrote on the methods of prayer, which often begin with *metanoia*, to make repentance or confession. Jesus taught that repentance was necessary as the first step toward following God, the Father.[9] McGuckin connects repentance to an act of becoming authentic. This is the actual translation of *metanoia*—to become authentic in an act of surrendering the ego to God or to admit one's errors or flaws in the beginning (or continuation) of a purification process toward a true state of *hesychia* and communion with God. It helps to be in a place of stillness and solitude to practice repentance, and nature is a perfect location.

Peace may be found in an isolated place like a desert, but also in the quiet and stillness of mountain forests. Much later, after the fourteenth and fifteenth centuries yet in the same tradition of the fourth-century Desert Fathers and Mothers of Egypt, monks and nuns of Eastern Europe withdrew to the desert for solitude and prayer. They were fleeing the invasions of the Turks in 1453, but also fleeing civilization in general. According to Andrew Louth and George Fedotov, the Egyptian and Syrian people's fourth-century withdrawal to the desert was "a reaction to the establishment of Christian society, whereas the Slavic people's fourteenth-century search for the forest was a flight from a disintegrating society."[10] They also assert that this marked a change from urban monasticism to a "renewal of the quest for the desert, rather than the discovery of monasticism itself."[11]

The forest is a place of spiritual experience and source of religious renewal, like the desert. This is due to the pure and unchanging nature

9. For New Testament teachings on repentance, see Matt. 4:17; Mark 1:4, 15; Luke 5:32; 2 Cor. 7:9-10.

10. Louth, *The Wilderness of God*, 123–24.

11. Ibid.

of Orthodoxy and of Orthodox monasticism; the desert tradition combined with Hellenic philosophy infused Byzantium, which carried *hesychia* "unto the ages of ages." The peace and solitude of the desert boulders, sand, and air are alive in the moss, ferns, and trees of the forests for all time. Nature was and always will be a place of true connection with God and the perfect place of prayer.

In the forests of northern Romania at Sâmbăta de Sus Monastery in Transylvania, the late Archimandrite Theofil Pârâian, the blind scholar and *starets*, also believes that prayer offers peace, but in a different way. When someone prays, he says, what is happening is that we "are making a house for Him in our heart." The presence of God our heavenly Father in us brings us peace. We can then say, as Archimandrite Theofil Pârâian does, "[F]or you are all, God. You are the emperor of our peace and our souls. You are holy and wholly our God. For you are our holiness. For yours is to save and have mercy on us. For you are a God of mercy and of love for humankind." Then we are never alone, and we need never fear anything because we are sanctified. God becomes our protector, our foundation for our whole life. "The love of God [is in us] because God is love in love, in His own essence."[12]

The archimandrite says that we can petition God and communicate with God directly. "I asked help from God and God [cannot possibly] to refuse me. So I'm not searching for independence in prayer, I'm searching, on the contrary, for a dependence on Christ Jesus. . . . I am still very strong on this point; that God will never abandon you when you ask for his help."[13] With or without a spiritual guide, God is available.

"To make a link between prayer and mind, between mind and heart, between the power that thinks and the power that loves," is the main purpose of prayer, which brings true peace, says Parinte Theofil. "The mind that goes down into the heart is not an activity of the human being; it is a work of God. What we are doing is that we pray to

12. Recorded January 21, 2007. HD Master Reels 28–29.

13. This English translation is rather fragmented, due to the subject's short, staccato speech patterns. The translation was done live while the *Parinte* (Father) was speaking, unlike others in this study that were done later.

God for the unity of our own being, the whole being." Archimandrite Theofil makes reference to and rejection of the Platonic notion of body, intellect, and soul. Plato portrayed the human condition as the mind/intellect in control over the body; through the virtue of intellect we reach God. To Theofil, we begin with the heart, where we find God, which brings a kind of indescribable peace that then informs the mind and intellect.

God, to Parinte Theofil, is primarily love; a greater love than the love found in human beings. God is with us, and loves us more than we love ourselves or anyone or anything. God consecrates and sanctifies us.

However, there is also a cautious tone that is present in this old blind monk. When one first starts petitioning God with prayer, the toxins of the soul can rise to the surface and become quite intimidating.

> [W]hen I started saying, "Jesus Christ Son of God," I have actually met the [dirt] of my own soul, and I was frightened. I couldn't imagine that in my soul one could find so much wickedness, so much bad loathing, which I wouldn't expect to find in my soul. And I wouldn't even make myself conscious that I have it, if I didn't look after my soul through the engagement in prayer. I always tell the people whom I recommend to say this prayer, not to get frightened when they discover how much dirt is in their own souls, which should be eliminated, and which does not vanish all of a sudden.

When this happens, his recommendation is to not give up, but rather stay the course and keep all concentration on God. As an aside, after the cameras were powered off, Parinte Theofil said: "The terrors of the soul will come, and that's when most people give up and abandon their practice." This is the most important moment. One must not give in to the demonic fears. Staying faithful despite the terror within the soul is how true spiritual depth of character is built. It was as if he was saying that God is found in experiencing the fear and terror inside one's self.

The import of the archimandrite's caution is that peace of mind and heart is only one aspect of life, and when it comes to *hesychia*, "facing one's demons" and going through a process of seeing negative aspects of the soul is one of the first steps. It is to be expected that when beginning a practice of the search for peace in silence and stillness, the *logismoi* will enter in by default. Learning to tame the "demons" of mental and physical distraction is itself the practice. The exercise of returning again and again to God inside the self, ignoring the fears and distracting desires, is what it means to practice *hesychia*.

Even farther north in the remote forests of Transylvania, in an area that since the eighteenth century has been called Bucovina, meaning "the country of beech trees," there is a convent named Voronet, famous for its fresco paintings of the Last Judgment on the church walls created in 1547.[14] Abandoned from 1785 until 1991 due to annexation by the Hapsburg Empire, the convent was recovered and is now run by Mother Superior Irina Pântescu. She is credited with reopening the monastery after 206 years of neglect. She turned it into a convent, raised significant funds, and established a monastery-based company run by the sisters producing candles, incense, and icons so that it may be financially self-sufficient. This woman has made a huge contribution to others and to Orthodox monasticism.

The abbess generously allowed an interview to be filmed on the subjects of peace, God, and *hesychia*. Asked what it means to experience peace in a spiritual way, Mother Superior Irina responded that if a woman or man prays, they are automatically peaceful and with God.

> Jesus said that the first commandment is to love God out of all your soul and your thoughts, and the second command as important as that one, to love your neighbor as yourself. . . . As long as God himself is peace, joy, silence, quietness, then a woman or man who loves God . . . loves peace, joy, silence, and loves her neighbor. She's actually promoting peace.

She went on to explain that the essence of a human being is actually the image or likeness of God.[15] To her, this "likeness of God" is the human

---

14. A deeply saturated blue color in art, "Voronet Blue" is named for the fresco on the church walls of this monastery, which some call the "Sistine Chapel of the East."

soul itself, which is the essence or core of each person. Once we realize this, peace becomes a natural condition, and love between neighbors is possible. "This is the essence of love," she explained. "One way or another we love peace, we love God who out of love for humankind has sent his only Son to be given for our redemption. And greater love than that there is [none] as for Christ to have laid down his own life for the salvation of the world."[16]

---

15. This is reminiscent of Genesis, St. Paul, Clement, Irenaeus, and Macrina's concepts of the "image" and "likeness" of God.

16. Recorded January 24, 2007. HD Master Reel 39.

PART II

Silence *(Hesychia)* in Contemporary Focus: Methodology and Importance of the Practices inside and outside Monasteries

---

As I have discussed in the introduction and history section of this book, *Hesychia* has two definitions: (1) a positive method of silence, stillness, and prayer, which may through God's grace instill (2) a state of spiritual connection and peace in those who practice it. Being in communion with God through private and shared practices of *hesychia* and public worship practices of the liturgy and Holy Eucharist offer monks and nuns individual and communal peace. In the previous section, I have provided several examples of experiences and methodologies of *hesychasts* throughout the ages.

In Part Two, I offer descriptions of the fruits of *hesychia* and its uses by contemporary practitioners in selected monasteries in Egypt, Mt. Sinai, Greece, and Romania. I describe new ways these contemporary *hesychasts* are modeling peace, compassion, and peaceful coexistence to others outside of monasteries.

Through combined use of narrative text and ethnographic film, a new method of transmission is being employed for the first time to introduce *hesychia*. Traditionally, texts, modeling, and mentor/disciple relationships exclusive to monasteries have been the pedagogical vehicles for instruction in *hesychia*. With this book and the companion film, high-definition ethnographic film and audio have recorded *hesychasts* describing and demonstrating their spiritual practices and life experiences inside monasteries in combination with the transcribed words from these recordings.

This book illustrates the importance and usefulness of these practices for those readers and viewers inside and outside monasteries and churches to connect with God, and to potentially experience peace and nonviolence through these ancient practices for themselves.

The final section of this essay will forward two arguments in the words and actions of the contemporary practitioners in the locations where I have focused this research. They are as follows:

> 1. Ancient and contemporary methods of *hesychia* provide peace and connection to God for the individual monk or nun.
> 2. These methods of *hesychia* may provide models of peace, compassion, peaceful coexistence, and the ways of connection to God for others outside monasteries.

These arguments are intended to present *hesychia* persuasively as both a practice and a state of being. While not instructional tools, the text and film are intended to encourage readers to explore *hesychia* for themselves and to add substantive material to the fields of theology, religious studies, religious art and architecture, and the field of media arts, among others, material that has previously not been available.

Used almost exclusively for almost two thousand years in Christian Orthodox monasteries and convents, *hesychia* has been described in many primary ascetic instruction manuals and biographies and in secondary analytical commentary. Now, contemporary *hesychia* is being studied and shared both inside and outside monasteries with scholars and nonascetics for the purpose of modeling peace and nonviolence in a troubled world through both traditional and alternative media.

If ever there was a need for peace, the time is now. As of this writing there are forty-two conflicts or major wars in progress.[1] War continues in the Middle East. Israel and Palestine dispute boundaries and endure constant civil unrest; there are bombs and acts of martyrdom on a daily basis. In 2006, there were 14,000 terrorist-related attacks resulting in approximately 20,000 deaths. Osama bin Laden, now deceased, the former leader of the terrorist group Al Qaeda, had tens of thousands of volunteers willing to martyr themselves in the name of God.[2] America is still involved in military operations in Iraq and Afghanistan. Africa has had more than twenty major wars since 1960, particularly in Rwanda, Somalia, Angola, Sudan, Liberia, and Burundi. Most of these conflicts or wars are civil or "intrastate" issues due to religious, racial, or ethnic differences. Many churches and monasteries have been pillaged and destroyed, or turned into mosques or temples of other religions.

The ways in which wars are fought have changed dramatically in the last two decades. Wars are no longer just fought by airplanes with bombs and missiles. There is little or no ground combat. Now the threat of terrorism generates fear, a kind of psychological fear-based, personal war. Conflicts and wars are now far more secretive, insidious, and individualized. There is constant fear in many people that at any moment an I.E.D., dirty nuclear bomb, or biological device may be triggered even in cities not actively at war. "Sleeper cells" of terrorists exist in America and in almost every major country in the world, ready to strike. The threat of nuclear war is real; in the last few years Pakistan,

1. http://www.globalsecurity.org/military/world/war/index.html

2. Washington Institute for Near East Policy and National Counterterrorism Center (NCTC), http://www.washingtoninstitute.org/templateC05.php?CID=2604.

North Korea, and possibly Iran have been added to the already long list of countries with nuclear weapons.

The monasteries included in this book are in these dangerous, war-torn areas of the Middle East, Africa, and Eastern Europe. Gently living in caves and monasteries on the edges of war zones, sheltered away from conquests and destruction in inner worlds of contemplation, peaceful Christian sages have lived for thousands of years and survived multiple threats of conquests, invasion, and wars. Yet, a few ancient monasteries, *sketes*, and places of safety remain: the monks and nuns have endured in these places for centuries. They practice and continually pray for peace in age-old monasteries: St. Antony's in Egypt is from the fifth century, and still functioning. St. Catherine's Monastery at the foot of Mt. Sinai has survived since the sixth century. The monasteries of Mt. Athos have survived over a thousand years. The ways of peace inside these remaining monasteries, and love for their neighbors, are the focus of this book.

What is it like for these monks and nuns to truly experience profound peace, and to be with God? Contemporary *hesychasts* in these warring areas now offer us the ancient methods of profound peace for those unable to pursue the life of an ascetic.

Peace, compassion, and coexistence through *hesychia*, wherever it is now practiced, began in the desert. For Christian monks and nuns, the desert is the fertile ground of peace. As it was some two thousand years ago, the desert is still a perfectly quiet and desolate place for worship and asceticism, and remains one of the great centers of *hesychia* despite the conflicts, war, and terrorism that surround them. Somehow through the vicissitudes of the harsh desert life the monasteries and the ascetics have not only survived, but through their faith and dedication to God they thrive.

5

On the Experience of Communication with God through *Hesychia*

As one might expect, the monks and nuns interviewed in the ethnographic study for this book all spoke about the importance of prayer in their practice of *hesychia*. Specifically, the Jesus Prayer, or an abbreviated variation, *Kyrie eleison* (Lord have mercy) is central and constant in their lives, allowing them to become silent and still and to experience a presence of God, a communication with him.

The Arabic word *salah* ("to make a connection") is used in Coptic Christianity to mean prayer and is also found in the Qur'anic Arabic language as *salawah*, a ritual prayer practiced by Muslims in surrender to Allah (God). In the Bosnian language, Našinski, and the Macedonian and Turkic languages it is commonly known by the term *namaz*, an Indo-European word meaning to bow or prostrate.

Two priests of St. Antony's Monastery talk about prayer. Sitting at the tomb of St. Antony, Father Ruwais explains, "*Salah*, the most expressive word in Arabic, means touching or conducting something or connecting with someone . . . with God. . . . In English [prayer] means pleading, or asking for something."[1] Prayer is essential to *hesychia*. It connects the monk or nun to God, and it is often used as the vehicle for ascetics to become silent.

---

1. Recorded January 18, 2007, Red Sea area, Egypt. HD Master 20.

Father Lazarus, the *starets* of St. Antony's Monastery, says this of the Jesus Prayer:

> The Jesus Prayer is the heart of God. And in this, you are silent. Because you have stilled all your passions. [You say in a whisper or internally] "Lord Jesus Christ have mercy on me." [or] "Lord Jesus Christ, son of God, have mercy on me, a sinner." Short form or the long form. Doesn't matter . . . Now this prayer, when you repeat it many times, when you use it as a prayer rule, as a discipline, because you use the same words repeated, and because it focuses on the name of Jesus, this prayer starts to diminish, not accelerate your thoughts. For example, when you pray the Jesus Prayer with concentration, with intention, with love, with humility, with penitence in your heart, you acknowledge something [or someone greater] when you are saying "Lord." You are calling Him, addressing somebody greater than you.
>
> Jesus. There is no other name by which you can be saved. He is the savior. Christ. He is the anointed one, God anointed him. God made him the one to save us. Lord Jesus Christ. You are already in a whole theology; you have moved in three words. You are way past your personal life into Jesus. "Have mercy on me, I need mercy."
>
> If you add your breathing . . . if you breathe in . . . "Lord Jesus Christ," you take in, you breathe in with your breath the name of the Lord, and you hold it, when you confess your sins, as Peter confessed you are the Lord, you confess your sins, you breathe in. And the result? You breathe out your sin. This is a marriage of body and soul. This is a purification of your body by your prayer. It's already an accelerated way of silence, because you arrive at a point where your mind is still because it has surrendered to Jesus.

These men are teaching their use of *hesychasm* in prayer that originated in Egypt and the Holy Lands, and later in Greece and Slavic lands. The exact origins of the Jesus Prayer are controversial: some scholars say it began with Jesus himself recommending his apostles to call on the name of God, "Father," or "Lord" directly.[2] Others say that in the fourth century, "arrow" prayers to Jesus were uttered. In the sixth century with St. John Cassian and St. Diadochos, it was thought that repetition of the name Jesus led to inner stillness. Others argue that the Jesus Prayer began with the late sixth-, early seventh-century abbot of St. Catherine's Monastery, St. John Climacus, in his recommendation to repeat the name of Jesus in continual prayer.

Father Lazarus adds the Athonite theology of St. Gregory Palamas and St. Gregory of Sinai, connecting breathing with the repetition of the name of Jesus, with the head bowed and the lungs compressed. The long-form ending of repentance, "a sinner" after "have mercy on me," was added later by an unknown Russian *hesychast*.[3] At Mt. Athos, this method of bowing the head and linking the Jesus Prayer to breathing has been in practice since the late thirteenth and early fourteenth centuries.

Since then, monasteries on Mt. Athos have experienced cycles of extremes, from thriving to near-extinction. The nineteenth and early twentieth centuries saw several monasteries close and many fall into severe states of disrepair. Those problems, however, are now in the past.

A contemporary Athonite monk, Elder Joseph the Hesychast (1898–1959) is credited with resurrecting Mt. Athos in Greece, the Holy Mountain, and six of its monasteries from decades of decline. The organizational success of this one unworldly and unschooled man, who isolated himself for decades, teaches us much about *hesychia*, its role in the Orthodox experience, and the relaying of the experience of direct communication with God in the Palamite tradition to his protégés.

---

2. "Hitherto you have asked nothing in My Name; ask and you will receive, that your joy may be full" (John 16:23).

3. According to John McGuckin. The addition of "a sinner" could also be from Luke 18:9-14, in the Pharisee and the Publican parable where the tax collector pleads, "God, be merciful on me the sinner!" (*NRSV*) There is also a very helpful distillation of the history and usage of the Jesus Prayer on the St. Vladimir's Orthodox Theological Seminary's website. An article, *Saying the Jesus Prayer*, by Albert S. Rossi may be found at http://www.svots.edu/Faculty/Albert-Rossi/Articles/Saying-the-Jesus-Prayer.html.

Elder Joseph the Hesychast propagated the theology of St. Gregory Palamas and that of the spiritual masters found in *The Philokalia*. The present abbot of the Holy Monastery of Vatopedi, Archimandrite Ephraim, is a protégé of Elder Joseph and describes his mentor and *geron* as "a contemporary witness of the supernatural charisma of the Holy Spirit in the Church."[4] In true Athonite fashion, the elder was full of love for the Holy Virgin Mary, the *Theotokos*, or Mother of God. He learned to become dispassionate toward worldly things through his devotion to the process of *apatheia*, to experience "love" for God from the words and guidance of the Fathers.

Elder Joseph the Hesychast and Elder Joseph both gave Mt. Athos and Athonite monasticism a renewed focus on acquiring the virtues, on constant prayer, and the return to discipline of the *nous*. They were current and articulate models of what it means to be a *hesychast* and the inner rewards of a life of *hesychia*.

Elder Joseph the Hesychast spoke of becoming "illuminated," an experience that he described as interrupting prayer and offering frequent *theorias*: rapture of *nous*, suspension of senses, stillness, silence of all body elements, and a union of God and human into one. This is attained through management of passions (*apatheia*), endurance of temptations, unending struggles, and ultimate exchange of the material for the immaterial.

In one of his letters, Elder Joseph the Hesychast wrote:

> So when grace abounds in a person and he knows all that we have written, he attains great simplicity; his *nous* expands and has great joy and has great capacity . . . it comes, like a subtle breeze, like a mighty gust of fragrant wind[5] overflows throughout the body, and the prayer stops; the bodily members cease to move, and only the *nous* is in *theoria* within an extraordinary light. A union of God and

---

4. Elder Joseph the Hesychast, *Elder Joseph the Hesychast: Struggles, Experiences, Teachings (1898-1959)*, 4th ed. (Karyes, Athos, Greece: Great and Holy Monastery of Vatopedi, 1999), 14.

5. Cf. Acts 2:2.

man occurs. . . . It is also like wax which melts when it approaches fire; it cannot remain in its natural state.[6]

Elder Joseph the Hesychast set himself the goal of praying the Jesus Prayer noetically. Initially, all he knew to do was to say it orally, and with the voice of his intellect rather than his soul. He tried for two years, he wrote, sitting every afternoon in the wilderness for two to three hours, crying inconsolably "until the dirt became mud with my tears." He kept appealing to *Panagia*[7] and the Lord to learn how to say the Prayer noetically, "as the Saints say it in *The Philokalia*." One day, at sunset, starved and weeping, he collapsed.

> I was looking at the church of the Transfiguration on the summit, beseeching the Lord. Then it seemed to me that a "mighty gust" of wind came from there which filled my soul with an ineffable fragrance. Immediately, my heart began like a clock to say the prayer noetically. So I got up, full of grace and infinite joy, and went inside the cave. There I bent my chin upon my chest and began to say the prayer noetically. As soon as I said the prayer a few times, I was at once raptured to *theoria*. Even though I was inside the cave and the door was closed, I found myself outside in heaven, in a wondrous place with profound silence and serenity of soul—perfect repose.[8]

What Elder Joseph the Hesychast is describing is the perfect state of *hesychasm*. He had integrated all parts of his being—physical, intellectual, the psyche, and *nous*. His practice of the Jesus Prayer and of silence and stillness had become automatic and completely integrated into his life. This is not only a state of perfect peace and connection with God; it is a transcendent reality beyond words or materiality into another plane of immortality. It sounds as if he had achieved salvation

---

6. Joseph the Hesychast, *Monastic Wisdom: The Letters of Elder Joseph the Hesychast*, 182–83. Also a reference to Gregory of Nyssa.

7. *Theotokos*, the Virgin Mother.

8. Joseph the Hesychast, *Monastic Wisdom: The Letters of Elder Joseph the Hesychast*, 193.

while still a human being living in a fallen world of corruption, illusion, and idolatry.

To Elder Joseph the Hesychast, monasticism is the highest form of human beings' attempts to accept the love of God. "To respond to the love of God who yearns to bestow His divinization upon man, making him like Himself, man would in fact become a small God possessing all the qualities of God Himself, the same glory, the same blessedness; identical in everything except His Essence . . ."[9] This is the ultimate and timeless goal of the *hesychast*.

Later in Egypt at the foot of Mt. Sinai two monks at St. Catherine's Monastery made mention of their connection with God, showing more examples in the practice of *hesychia*.

When I asked what communing with God was like, Elder Pavlos, the *geron*, said, like others in this survey, that the vehicle to God is prayer.

> Prayer is the breath of the heart. It is the mouth of heaven, of paradise. It is the mouth of the angels. When we pray we are actually similar to the angels who are in a state of ceaseless praise for God. Therefore, we are told that prayer should be ceaseless.
>
> Therefore, if we are always in prayer, ceaselessly praising God, we are always with God.

In contrast, while we were filming at St. Catherine's, Father Nilus, the lowest monk at St. Catherine's, still a novice and not yet tonsured, was made a priest after seven years of apprenticeship. He is truly a practicing *hesychast*. It is fitting to have filmed Father Nilus's first Eucharist as a priest, although he was most embarrassed and felt he had made many errors.[10] He did not wish to speak about his Eucharistic service, out of true humility, but spoke extensively on *hesychia*.

9. Joseph the Hesychast, *Elder Joseph the Hesychast: Struggles, Experiences, Teachings (1898-1959)*, 11.

10. See the documentary portion of this book. The Divine Liturgy of St. John Chrysostom is conducted by Father Nilus, his first as a full priest.

"I think God is always present, and that's something that I'm always aware of. It's a bit like a prayer of words, but it is a silence. I think my relationship with God is in these words: 'Lord have mercy on me, a sinner.'" Christ to this priest is everything, "alpha and omega," as he says. A former British heir who abandoned great wealth, the novice finds richness in God, in Christ, in silence, in the life of a *hesychast*, through prayer and struggle.

> I think if we search for God, God's providence guides us in which direction to go. In many ways it's the sorrows of this life that open up prayer for us.
>
> It is like when Christ said, "Those who love the world hate me, and those who hate the world love me." We know that the Gospels not only reveal the state of time and moment, but they reveal the state of man's world outside the garden of paradise. It's like St. Augustine said, "If we look at the world around us it's like a vale of tears."[11]

I was not told of Father Nilus's personal sorrows, but they are visible in his humility. He was the quietest monk of all, always sitting way off in a corner, head bowed, in prayer. He did not tell me that he had renounced his family's wealth; another monk informed me. Because of the apparent depth of his devotion to God and his total love and dedication to *hesychasm*, he is included at the monastery and also here among the influential *hesychasts*.

Another lover of God but living in total solitude, as differentiated from all the other monks in this book, is elderly Father Makarios,[12] at the seventeenth-century Monastery of the Taxiarches (Archangels) on the little Greek island of Serifos. I include him and the little monastery of Taxiarches as a contrast to the other monasteries in this essay: it is the newest (built around 1600) and has the fewest in its community (one). In contrast to contemporary Athonite monasteries, Taxiarches was once thriving with lots of monks and regular services, "but they all got old and died, and were never replaced," Father Makarios tells us.

11. Recorded January 16, 2007, Mt. Sinai. HD Master Reel 13.
12. The name Makarios means "blessed" in Greek.

This lone monk gives tours, hears confessions, presides over special feasts, conducts vespers and matins twice a week (mostly by and for himself), and occasionally assists in Sunday liturgy in town, in the *hora*. He raises all his own food, with a large garden and chicken coop, and does all the cleaning and maintenance work himself. Father Makarios generously granted us an on-camera interview and tour of the monastery. He told me later that he felt it was important to teach people, both Orthodox and others, about God.

Father Makarios's practice of *hesychia* is pure and simple: he is alone most of the time, and his life is by default composed of silence and stillness. He has very few visitors, perhaps only five or so per day, mostly tourists uninterested in spiritual guidance. The other island priest usually conducts the one liturgy performed on the island each week, at the main church in the center of the village. This leaves Father Makarios with much time on his hands for prayer and contemplation of God and his graces.

Father Makarios's practice of *hesychia* is that of action. He connects God through prayer with everything he does. He says, "Peace and love are only passages of thought. I find *hesychia* with my actions; in doing what God wants me to do." When he talks to people, he feels that he is talking to God. When he works in his garden or in his fields, planting, weeding, tilling, watering, he is praying to God. He sings psalms in his garden and sings and chants while cleaning, sweeping, mopping, and doing laundry. Yet, despite his solitude he says he is a very happy and satisfied man. Like St. Antony, Father Makarios is "entombed." Of course he can come and go at will, but claims he has everything he needs at Taxiarches, so he stays there. Most of his life is in silence, with only the sound of the sea and winds whistling through the monastery.

Father Makarios's practice is entirely faith-based. He does not see or feel God, yet he constantly offers himself to a God unseen, a divine presence, and feels a kind of indescribable love in return. He puts himself aside to do God's work. He worries about nothing, relying entirely on God's grace. He knows that God is real, and does not need logic or proof for reassurance. Father Makarios's faith in God is not only the *ousia* of his core being, his faith is his identity. Father Makarios is a lover in love with God; you can see it in his eyes and in his smile. You can see his faithful love of God in his work: the monastery is impeccably kept and beautiful. Several citizens of Serifos tell me that he is the kindest and friendliest person on the island. This is his faithful love of God reflected in his relationships with the people, the monastery, and the island. He is truly a disciple and apostle of Christ.

As the monastery is in a state of dwindling repair and there is little money to keep it going, it is hard for a single monk to maintain it all himself, yet he does. He does not know what will happen to it when it comes time for him: "The patriarch [from Athens] will decide." He is not worried. He has "never regretted" his choice to become a monk and priest and has lived in this monastery for forty-eight years. He offers love, but has also received much love, he says. "There is nothing I can say to describe monastic life and *hesychia*. It can only be experienced. Nothing is more beautiful than to pay full attention to God."

He is the one monk discussed in this book who has no spiritual father as mentor; God directly is his counselor, he says. Father Makarios and the other priest in the village do not spend much time together; I was told they don't get along well with one another because the other priest is "unfriendly," an impression I shared after meeting him.

In short, Father Makarios living alone with God at the Monastery of the Taxiarches on Serifos says to the rest of the world that God provides for all needs. We do not need much else. A good life may be sustained with very few material goods and lots of faith.

6

Hesychia as a Model for Those Outside Monasteries

As I established in the beginning of this section, there is a great need for peace in the world between religions and nations, in individuals, and for peaceful coexistence with neighbors of all cultures and traditions as well. While this is a time of conflict, war, and terrorism, it is also a time of isolation, loneliness, and economic hardship for many people.

At the same time there is a new trend indicating great interest in religious education, practical training, and spiritual self-help, in *ascesis*.[1] This is the case not only for monks and nuns, but also for the general public outside of monasteries. Many people are engaged in mentorship and pastoral care in churches, social and psychological therapies, spiritual guidance in books and emerging self-help media. There is a large, hungry audience for spiritual and religious books, videos, audio, and in films. In the United States alone, $9.6 billion dollars were spent in 2005 on such items.[2] What these "consumers" are looking for is personal liberation, growth, health, and peace of mind, through worship and spiritual practices.

These desires for peace and peaceful coexistence may be served through mystical literacy and spiritual practices in historic and relatively unknown and underappreciated Christian practices of silence and contemplation: through *hesychia*. Once restricted to faraway monasteries in relatively inaccessible places like the deserts of Egypt,

1. Nineteenth-century Greek, *askesis*, or "training," from *askein*, "to exercise."
2. Marketdata Enterprises, 2005.

Africa, or the forests of Eastern Europe, these living traditions are now available to help people in their desire to experience something deeper and more fulfilling: a connection to God.

Much of mystical Christianity found in faraway monasteries has been mistakenly believed to be strange or punishing. Lives of monks and nuns have sometimes carried connotations of escapism or arduous, punishing obedience, as some archimandrites and abbots, such as Pachomius and St. Basil, were quite strict. Others, such as St. Antony, subjected themselves to stringent or even self-punishing lifestyles, at least to the outside observer. Liturgies are often thought of as dry and interminably long. Doctrines and dogma have become negative words to many, perceived as offensively dry, impossibly moral, officious, and authoritarian. The reality, in my view, is exactly the opposite. The majority of the monks and nuns that I met in my research were delightfully joyous, energetic, and full of spirit and love. Liturgies and Eucharistic rituals were celebrations of liberation and enlightenment. Monasteries are not only peaceful refuges; they are centers of new vitality and personal growth and healing.

Ancient Christian ascetic practices are brimming with life and energy and are available to people to be integrated into modern life—without having to leave one's work and family and become a sequestered monk or nun. There is growing interest: St. Catherine's Monastery receives almost three hundred visitors per day; Varatic, Agapia, and Voronet convents have thousands of visitors each summer. Interest in "pilgrimages" to Mt. Athos has never been stronger.

There are philosophical and theological paths to self-realization and connection with God available in ancient Christian practices of *hesychia*. The quest for inner fulfillment and peace is alive and well in contemporary monasteries, and it is time to bring them into urban and suburban modernity for the purpose of uniting people, freeing them from self-inflicted isolation, overconsumption, and reliance on temporal, material objects. The practice of the Jesus Prayer, contemplation in silence, spending time in stillness in nature or in sacred places at home or work, can revive and repair the inner self, helping to restore a person to full aliveness, creative expression, and profound peace.

By adapting the ancients' methods of *hesychia* and *hesychasm* and practicing them in limited ways in the context of daily life, the heart and soul can be cleansed and spiritually fulfilled. Prayer and meditation can lift the psyche and soul into mystical realms of divine connection. We can unite with the image and likeness of God inside each of us, and stop our own self-destructive beliefs and acts. We can unite with others and appreciate differences instead of annihilating them.

Peace as Ecumenical Dialogue

The spirit of peace through ecumenism and interreligious dialogue is beginning to bloom. This has been very unpopular to strict adherents of Orthodox traditions but encouraging to those of us who are not and can never become monks or nuns. A living example of the new ecumenical spirit, controversial or not, is the former Metropolitan and new patriarch of the Romanian Orthodox Church, His Beatitude Patriarch Daniel Ciobotea, who generously gave me an extended interview just before he was elected as patriarch.

Considered a new, scholarly, and compassionate voice in contemporary Eastern Orthodox Church practices in the former Communist country of Romania, His Beatitude Patriarch Daniel Ciobotea is known for his many publications and his commitment to open the church to new believers, particularly young people. His analysis and commentary on the Trinity are also notable and exciting.

Since our interview, His Beatitude has become the new patriarch of the Romanian Orthodox Church; when I filmed him in January 2007, he was the Metropolitan of Moldavia and Bucovina.[3] He spoke on-camera of the ultimate truth of God through Holy Communion, in a Trinitarian perspective. To His Beatitude, the Triune God is our source; we achieve unity with the Father through the Holy Spirit and the conduit of the Son. This is effected in material form through the Eucharist, or Holy Communion. Patriarch Daniel teaches that the ascetic life and the life within the Orthodox Church should not be

---

3. He was installed as the Patriarch after the passing of His Beatitude Patriarch Theoctist in August 2007. Both persons were filmed as part of this project, but are not included in the ethnographic field video due to time constraints. I plan to ultimately publish their full interviews, in text and video, on a website.

primarily seen as a life of obedience, servitude, or uniformity. Rather, the vehicles of God and Christ and the church should be conduits of liberation and freedom—of coordination, not subordination, in fellowship. His Beatitude further believes that "the Church is primarily called to be the eschatological consciousness of the world and of the entire Creation, the sacramental icon and foretaste of the Kingdom of God, the laboratory of the Resurrection."[4]

The new Romanian patriarch's position is that a life of obedience to the church, with faithful attention to *hesychastic* and liturgical practices, can be joyful, positive, and eternally life-affirming. Further, the world and the church are material for God to enact a shift not only in consciousness, but in an eschatological sense and in the sense of personal, individual resurrection. This is a marked differentiation from other Orthodox leaders' views that the world is fallen and needs to be subdued. His is a new voice in *hesychasm*, an expansion of the Orthodox Church by opening the doors of monastic mystical practices to others.

I asked him if it is necessary to be a monk or nun or to live in a monastery to experience communion with God. His Beatitude answered:

> I think the very important meaning of prayer is that we can pray everywhere, not only in the desert. And today some great cities, big cities, the megalopolis are similar to the desert, not because there are not many people in them but certain similarity is given by the feeling of solitude. Although there are crowds of people, many persons are feeling like [they are] in the desert because there is not enough communion, not enough communication and I think the prayer is to transform the solitude into communion, and first of all communion with God, fellowship with God.

---

4. Daniel (Metropolitan and Patriarch) Ciobotea, *Confessing the Truth in Love: Orthodox Perceptions on Life, Mission and Unity* (Iasi: Trinitas, 2001), 7–8.

This is a radical reimagining of the desert and its place in *hesychastic* relationship with God. What His Beatitude is saying is that many of us are already living in desert-like isolation even though we live in big cities or towns with many people. Why not transform our isolation into contemplation and prayer and make a connection with God? Why not join in fellowship with other seekers of inner-revelation and transformation, thereby uniting with others in spiritual sojourning, reconciliation, and redemption through Christ?

When I asked what we could do to experience God in the context of our day-to-day lives as ordinary, secular people, he said,

> . . . it's not necessary to live in the desert to be isolated from the world. What is important is to be united with God. Even in New York City, or in Bucharest, or in Iasi or in the village. . . . The important attitude is to remind us that we are in the presence of God. And to start to speak with him silently, not just by words. And this communion of our mind with God, it's the beginning of a good prayer, although we are in the cities, or we are working in the office. And it's a question of desire to meet God and to let God share in our life. And in this sense we can conclude then to say that the prayer is not only our activity, it is the activity also of God in us.

The election of His Beatitude Patriarch Daniel to the highest position in the Romanian Orthodox Church marks a new transition, and a renewal of ecumenical spirit in a country that is itself renewed after a period of extreme repression and hopelessness. Our work in Romania represented an opportunity to present and analyze a contemporary place where *hesychia* is alive and well, and where it has an actual future in the culture beyond the monasteries.

The Romanian Orthodox Church as it exists today is an amalgam of several groups that emerged in 1925, forming the "Patriarchate of the Romanian Church." It is the second largest of European Orthodoxy, with only Russia larger, according to Meyendorff.[5] Despite a "severe blow dealt by the secularization of monastic properties and the reforms which followed," monasticism in Romania recovered between World Wars I and II, and after the 1950s enjoyed a "renaissance."[6] This renewal took place in spite of the Communist Party rule of Nicolae Ceausescu between 1965 and his overthrow in 1989.

Peace by Loving God Obediently

Also in Romania, in the mountainous north in Maramure in an area known as Baia Mare, is a beautiful monastery called Rohia. There was a very old former *starets* there, the late Father Seraphim, who wisely advised us on how "ordinary people" can begin to find peace.

To Father Seraphim, it is important that we are always positive in everything we do in life. We are able to do this because we have a creator God that totally takes care of us at all times. No matter if we are carpenters, cab drivers, musicians, teachers, or business people, if we admit that we make mistakes, that we are sinners and live in a world of crime, mistreatment of others, poverty, and sin, if we do our best to remember God in all that we say and do, God will take care of us.

The care of God, to Father Seraphim, sometimes comes in ways we do not expect or find pleasant. Sometimes God's care seems like punishment. Often, we are attracted to behaviors and self-destructive acts; this, he says, is due to a weakness of faith, yet it is always possible to learn from our sins and errors. He explains, "We are weak in faith, we don't have faith, we don't have love for God. We don't have the basic needed love for our neighbor. And that keeps us astray from God. And going away from God means going away from happiness."[7]

The way for anyone to find peace and to be with God is to draw nearer to God. "It is therefore our duty, if we call ourselves Christians, to be honest, righteous people. And if we give homage to God He will come towards us to meet us with peace, with understanding, and with kindness."[8] This is true not only for monks and nuns, but for anyone.

5. John Meyendorff, *The Orthodox Church: Its Past and Its Role in the World Today* (Crestwood, NY: St. Vladimir's Seminary Press, 1981), 165.

6. Bishop Seraphim Joanta, *Romania: Its Hesychast Tradition and Culture*, trans. Pere Romul Joanta (now Bishop Seraphim of Fagaras), vol. 46, Spiritualité Orientale et Vie Monastique (Wildwood, CA: St. Xenia Skete, 1992), xvii.

7. Recorded January 22, 2007. HD Master Reel 22.

For Father Seraphim at Rohia Monastery in Romania today as for the late Athonite Elder Joseph the Hesychast, to love God is to keep God's commandments obediently, and to fulfill the will of the heavenly Father, just as Jesus was to the Father "obedient unto death, even unto death on a Cross" (Phil. 2:8). An effort to maintain the holy commandments of God is required. These were given by God not from on high, but from a place of equality with human beings, like Jesus Christ observing them himself in human form.[9]

Bishop Kallistos Ware writes that through love for God and love for others, one becomes "a magnet, a pole of attraction; the life becomes transparent, so that others are able to see Christ in and through him."[10] Then everything in life becomes about God, and with God, through God. Elder Joseph insisted that there is nothing without grace, and grace is never a reward but a gift from God.

Elder Joseph was a man of intense severity, denying himself in extreme ways yet never appearing to be depressed or unhappy, but "joyful and warm" with his disciples, according to Ware.[11]

Most importantly, his was a whole life of inner recollection, of stillness, *hesychia*, through prayer, specifically the Jesus Prayer—which he called "the prayer." He taught that "[o]bedience is the first thing that God our Creator requires from His creations, particularly those who are endowed with reason."[12] But obedience was not to him a product of reason or intellect; it was something deeper, at the core. It was the means by which humans become connected or reconnect with their Creator.

Elder Joseph taught that it was of vital importance to always be connected with God, the Creator. Total dependence on God was not only important, it was logical and practical. In counterpoint, to not be connected with God, or in other words to be disobedient, was

---

8. Ibid.

9. Joseph the Hesychast, *Elder Joseph the Hesychast: Struggles, Experiences, Teachings (1898-1959)*, 11–12.

10. Ibid., 17.

11. Ibid., 19.

12. Ibid., 216.

irrational. Being independent and disconnected would lead one to "corruption and death."[13]

Elder Joseph defined obedience to God as an act of love. The self must be put aside to care for the other. He said, "Practical love is impossible without submission. How is it possible to offer love and to serve others if you do not submit to the other's will? Every action of practical love is an act of service and therefore those who are obedient offer a double work: practical faith in the person who gives the command, and applied love through the service they offer."[14] This kind of obedience is not harsh or depriving or strict; rather, it is compassionate, gentle, and loving.

Elder Pavlos, the current *geron* of St. Catherine's Monastery, teaches us that finding peace and loving God requires attention and care. This is obedience, but in kinder and softer terms as he says,

> If it were impossible to achieve [peace] then God would not ask for it. It requires however attention (*prosohi*). That's the secret. In other words, man must be careful, both the monastic, as well as the person who lives in the world. Life in Christ is something internal not external. The person needs to tuck into his heart—that's where the secret lies and if the person can have internal peace then he will also have peace with the world around him.

So, to find peace and happiness in a fallen world filled with conflict, war, and a multitude of vicissitudes, it is up to us. We must put God into our heart and mind through careful attention and action.

His Eminence Archbishop Damianos takes this idea of *prosohi* further, indicating that both the external and internal must be responsibly cared for. The material world is combined inseparably with the spiritual world. Analogously, this is also true in the human body: we are composed of *theoria* (theory) and *praxis* (action-physical activity) inside the Father's (God's) house. We go in and out endlessly, between internal and external. It's a somewhat complicated concept of

13. Ibid., 217.
14. Ibid., 218.

duality, which he illustrates as a balance between good and evil, theory and action.

"I enter into the Father's house and oh, I feel so nice inside! Then comes the evil desire that pulls me out, and I become the prodigal son. Again I go in and again back out. This movement in and out will go on throughout our entire life. However, the shorter the distance between our 'out' position and our Father's house, the better off we are."

This in-and-out between good and evil, sin and divinity can be stilled through the sacrament of repentance, or confession, explains His Eminence Archbishop Damianos. The biggest secret is to never let yourself sink into one or the other attribute of existence. Never let yourself fall fully into despair, for "it is a sign of faithlessness." Never let yourself be totally full of yourself and think that you are perfect, as only God, the Father, is perfect. Either way there is no need for worry or hopelessness, as "Christ can forgive any and every sin we ever make,"[15] he assures us.

15. Recorded January 17, 2007. HD Master Reels 7 and 8.

7

Peace and Compassion through Prayer: A Union of Mind and Body

Mother Maria of Agapia Monastery in Transylvania says, like others, that the most important key to being a whole and peaceful person dedicated to God and humanity is to recite the Jesus Prayer. She thinks that everyone, not just tonsured nuns and monks, should say it. It is not easy, though, because "first of all, I am sinful. I am very conscious of my sinfulness." It is easier to say the prayer when you live in silence. She knows that for most people outside of monasteries, this is not possible. When she is in her cell, she can recite the prayer for long periods of time. For others, she recommends reciting it for only a quarter hour or so, or when it is convenient and there are no other duties to perform.

It is especially important to recite the Jesus Prayer "whenever you are troubled, or whenever you have emotions." Then God grants peace—the peace of the heart, "which is ineffable, you cannot speak of it. It is a gift of God, the grace of the Holy Spirit. And the Holy Spirit blows where he wishes."[1] The first step toward peace is repentance, which she defines as "hating the sin."

Then, do your best to place the prayer into your heart. "You strive yourself . . . to introduce the name of the Lord in your heart. You try, but it is difficult to find the place of the heart. It's not easy. And at the same time you could be deceived . . . even if you feel some warmth in the region [of the] heart." Again, the way back from deception is

---

1. Recorded January 24, 2007. HD Master Reel 37-4.

via repentance. She finished our interview as the evening vespers were about to begin singing "repentance, repentance, repentance!"

The late Archimandrite Theofil Pârâian, the blind scholar and *starets* at Sâmbta de Sus, has a totally different opinion of the Jesus Prayer. He claims that the prayer does not address the name of Jesus at all. "When somebody comes to me [and I ask if they pray] 'Jesus Christ Son of the Living God, have mercy on me the sinner,' they would answer me suddenly, 'Oh, that is the Jesus prayer,' and I say the prayer is not the Jesus prayer in the way [they think it is], in itself, because it doesn't say much about Jesus. But it is about the way you have to pray." It is a prayer like any other prayer, he says. It is not the prayer of Jesus (or Jesus praying); it is addressed to the Lord Jesus and is a way to invoke or request his mercy. It may be linked to breathing or any body position as the Athonites recommended, and "may be told anytime, anywhere." Actually, it is a prayer for the monk, not for Jesus. "It is a prayer by which the monks are saving themselves." And one difference between a monk and a layperson is that for the monk, praying the Jesus Prayer continually is obligatory. Not so for others.

> We know that the prayer is a dialogue between our mind and God. We shouldn't only ask something from God. We also have to praise God. We have to thank God. We must confess God, in front of God. And we have to tell him our wickedness, our helplessness. To ask his help in order to confess "there in confession." And to look after ourselves, hoping that God is with us.[2]

Parinte Theofil reminded us with a smile that it was the thief that was the first inheritor of heaven. "Jesus consecrated him, and made him worthy of heaven. In the same way he will welcome us, who are not thieves!" So there is no need to worry about being a sinner, as long as we admit the failing to Jesus and ask him for forgiveness.

Most seriously, Parinte Theofil explained that the purpose of prayer for the monastic and for laypersons is to "make a link between mind and heart, between the power that thinks and the power that

2. Recorded January 2007. HD Master Reels 25 and 28.

loves. . . . So the mind that goes down into the heart is not an activity of the human being. It is a work of God. What we are doing is that we pray to God for the unity of our own being, the whole being."[3]

BEYOND PRAYER TO *HESYCHIA*

Going beyond reason, inducing the Jesus Prayer into the body at the point of the lips, then into the heart, unites the mind and intellect as well, says Archbishop Iustinian of Baia Mare, Romania, in agreement with Archimandrite Theofil. Before doing so, however, it is necessary to lay all human thoughts and concerns aside, entering a sanctuary of silence and relinquishing the self: the practice of *hesychia*.

Archbishop Iustinian teaches that "[t]he main occupation of the Christian life is prayer. In order to pray normally a human being should get his inner silence. . . . St. Symeon the New Theologian has stated that reason is not what enlightens the human being but the pure heart, which is absolutely different. I don't mean by heart a simple, sentimental life. When the heart is pure it starts elevating itself towards the mind, and it enlightens the mind, and it goes slowly down on the lips, and then the human being says, 'Jesus Christ, Son of God, have mercy on me.' So it is the opposite side by which you proceed [from that beginning with reason]: from the heart towards the mind toward the lips."[4]

Both Parinte Teofil and Archbishop Iustinian are subscribing to the teaching of Diadochus of Photice—that the locus of God is in the heart. It may be the mind that chooses to begin the process, and the *nous* that receives the product, but it is the heart that is God's "home" to these two Romanian monks.

His Eminence also claims that the Jesus Prayer did not begin at Mt. Sinai with St. John Climacus. Rather, it began with Christ and the apostles directly, a gift from God in order to "begin a process of purity, which generates illumination, which leads to deification,"[5] of the human being who prays in silence.

---

3. Recorded January 21, 2007. HD Master Reels 25 and 28.
4. Recorded January 23, 2007. HD Master Reel 33.
5. Ibid.

I was surprised to hear the archbishop say that whenever he greets faithful Christians his only job is to put his hand on their heart and say, "'May you have a pure heart.' This is how I greet as a bishop. Through laying the hands on somebody's being you see his or her face enlightened. Because Christ does not come from reason . . ."[6]

The emphasis on heart rather than reason can seem like semantic or theological hairsplitting until one experiences it for oneself. I do not fully understand what happened to me when Archbishop Iustinian put his hand on my heart. I can only say that I felt cleansed and illuminated with a kind of pure radiance. Could I call it a Holy Communion with God? It felt divinely spiritual, certainly. I understood nothing of the words Archbishop Iustinian was saying to me in Romanian; later I was told that he looked into my eyes, put his hand on my heart, and said, "Some people have had inadequate fathering." How he knew that was true of my childhood, I will never know. Whatever happened, I felt like a newborn baby, fully alive and ready for a whole new life to come.

MODELS OF PEACEFUL COEXISTENCE

Father Seraphim of Rohia Monastery says that through prayer the church fathers have been in a ceaseless contemplation with God, and they realize by this that everything around us—the environment—is actually speaking about God, and that brings peace to the whole world. "When we see a little piece of land full of flowers we have to think, what are the regulations? What are the rules that have been put inside them that some of them are yellow, blue, green, red, or what gives them this immense power and the state to be, to have a different geometric form?"

He explains that those types of questions lead us to the thought of the goodness and the power, the endless power of God, as witnessed through creation. That witness of the Creator's creation and the inseparability of each leads us to start praising and praying to him so that he expands his kindness to us, to the whole inhabited world, and to the universe. Father Seraphim says of the liturgy and of *hesychia* that "our prayers should not be done for ourselves. Any prayer should be

6. Recorded January 23, 2007. HD Master Reel 33.

done for the whole world. In the liturgy we are praying for those in prison, for those sick, for those who are traveling."

> When I say a prayer I always think of the people who are in surgery, under a surgery, of those who are suffering, those who are traveling [by] air and many others. And the [potential] damage, to protect people against accidents, and for the peace and understanding of the world as a whole. We are praying for good order in the universe. We pray that God, that the earth bring fruits, so that its fruits should be taken in peace, understanding and in a good state of soul.

Therefore we see that the monasteries in our world are, as it were, oases for prayer, especially dedicated to prayer for the salvation and safety of others. The monks have left the world but then live in monasteries for the sake of the world. "So we seek not to go back into the world but to make the people come to us and find their peace. We pray and we try to empathize with all those who are in danger and suffering and in many dangers so that God protects them."[7]

Mother Superior Irinia of Voronet reminds us that the first commandment of Jesus Christ is to love God with all your soul and your thoughts, "and the second command is as important as that one, to love your neighbor as yourself."

She goes on to say eloquently that God is the source of all love, peace, silence, and stillness. If a woman or man loves this peace and joy in the silence and stillness of *hesychia*, she is actually promoting love between others—themselves lovers of God and of his peace. When we look deeply inside ourselves we find the love and peace of God there inside, as our essence. When we know our neighbor well, and love them, we also see that image of peace and God in them shining back to us as divine love.[8]

On Mt. Athos, a young monk, Father Matthew, an American from Wisconsin who had lived there about eight years, told me that he thought of Vatopedi Monastery and the Holy Mountain itself as

7. Recorded January 22, 2007. HD Master Reel 32.
8. Recorded January 22, 2007. HD Master Reel 39.

a "giant transmitter of prayer for the entire world." Few know about this, but it is powerful and is "on the air twenty-four hours a day, seven days a week for the last thousand years." Mt. Athos is a constant prayer broadcast network; it is invisible, but penetrates everything in the universe with prayer waves.[9]

Helping others find peace and divine connection is important to the sisters at Văratec as well. They are happy to accept visitors to the convent, and their hospitality has been traditional for many years. Some come for the services, the vespers and matins in their three churches; others come for peace; still others want to speak to the nuns to confess sins or ask for forgiveness. Abbess Josephina said,

> There are people from [all over] the world searching for hesychasts, for hermits, because they believe they find something in their lives, because they know that these are holy people, people of prayer. And this is why somehow we are keeping always the open gates of the monastery for the people . . . a support for the people who wanted to know God. When people are in search, they try to find a place for meditation, rest, and retreat. . . . We are pleased at this, because when we see people who find some answers, we feel that our struggle is not in vain, [that] we are useful to them. And that's a comfortable feeling.[10]

Abbess Josephina told me that most of all, "people are in a permanent search [for] each other, interestingly enough." It is a relationship with another person, such as a nun, someone who is dedicated to peace and helping others is the one whom most of their visitors want to bond with. While filming at Văratec, our crew was approached by several nuns who wanted to welcome us. One in particular, Sister Justine, a very old nun who had lived there for over seventy years, told me that she had "felt our presence . . ." from a distance; she sensed "the love that we had in trying to help others, and wanted to come immediately to meet and help us and encourage us in our work." She walked with

9. An aside to me, recorded in my written journal.
10. Recorded January 24, 2007. HD Master Reels 36-1 and 36-2 A/B.

us back to our van, explaining that it was God who had brought her there, and God who gives her everything she needs. It was God who will guide us in making this project available to many in need. This was the living spirit of loving God and neighbor.

8

Hesychia in Our Own Practice

"The spiritual teaching and the living tradition of Athos, the bearer of saints, has been flowing forth now for over a thousand years, refreshing the spiritual existence of every human being thirsting for God his Creator with the sweetest of spring waters," says Archimandrite Ephraim, abbot of Vatopedi Monastery on Mt. Athos. These spiritual teachings are available to those who do not live on Mt. Athos, too, as long as certain rules are observed. Archimandrite Ephraim is very strict in his teachings and insistence on monastic obedience, but at the same time, has a warm heart and encourages laypersons to seek guidance from God in their own ways.

OBEDIENCE TO THE COMMANDMENTS

As abbot of the second-oldest and largest of the Athonite communities, Archimandrite Ephraim bespeaks his love of God and of monasticism, which he feels is "the highest form of man's ascetic attempt to respond to the love of God Who yearns to bestow His divinization upon man, making him like Himself. Man would in fact become a small God possessing all the qualities of God Himself, the same glory, the same blessedness; identical in everything except His Essence . . ."[1]

The archimandrite is a strict believer and practitioner of the commandments of God as a "therapeutic cure for a complete recovery from the corruption of our nature," but it must be with a spiritual

1. Joseph the Hesychast, *Elder Joseph the Hesychast: Struggles, Experiences, Teachings (1898-1959)* 4th ed. (Karyes, Athos, Greece: Great and Holy Monastery of Vatopedi, 1999), 11–12.

guide. The commandments, he believes, are the method of communication between humans and God. We commune with God through obedience to the commandments, and to our elders and spiritual masters. This obedience comprises a true and total denial of the pleasures of the material—the "heroism of taking up the Cross of Christ," and abstention from the "demons" of the body and mind, to enjoy the "peace and calm given by the Holy Spirit to those who live in harmony with His commandments."[2] This is done by cleansing, through baptism, by ascetic means handed down by the fathers of the church, and by a return to the "normalcy of nature."

This latter condition, "the normalcy of nature," to Archimandrite Ephraim means total immersion in God and denial of the passions: the precondition of *hesychia*, a life of silence and prayer. The nature of the human being is spiritual; and it is a return to that original spiritual essence that is the point and goal of *hesychia*.

A Spiritual Guide

I asked Archimandrite Ephraim what the first step should be for both monks and lay Christians interested in *hesychia*. He stressed the necessity of following a spiritual guide in a person's quest to know God and to find God within themselves and in others. "Of the utmost importance is finding and obeying a spiritual leader," he told me. "You cannot and must not make your own ideas on following Christ." This coincides with the literature I've studied; almost every manual for ascetic practice warns against attempting the practice of *hesychia* alone. This caution is understandable: it's an entirely different matter to be a monk or nun and pray twenty to twenty-two hours per day than it is to live in modern society and to pray once a week on Sunday for an hour or two or before bedtime or to say grace before meals. Being a monk consists of a life devoted to God through prayer; secular life is about earning a living, fulfilling a mission, perhaps raising a family. God may be at the center of a secular life, but the practices of *hesychia* are not central and cannot be to someone who is not an ascetic. Those practices can be central only to someone who has renounced

2. Ibid., 12–13.

the secular life and become an ascetic, according to Archimandrite Ephraim.

Archimandrite Ephraim's cautions were not easy for me to hear. I came with a predisposition that one could speak and commune with God directly, and that an intermediary, be it a *geron* or *starets* or even Christ, was optional. I have since learned that a relationship between monk and spiritual father is as important today as it was in antiquity. The intermediary between the devotee and the teacher, and a relationship between God and man via the Eucharist, is key for the monk; it may also be helpful for the secular worshipper. A secular believer may pray while undertaking daily affairs, but that is "multi-tasking," not a practice of pure *hesychia*. It is important to have a spiritual guide in the form of a priest, nun, pastoral counselor, or deacon, so that one is not led astray by self-delusions. Otherwise, prayers and moments of *hesychastic* silence and stillness should be kept to a minimum—a few minutes at a time—certainly not for hours and hours.

Bishop Kallistos Ware explains that the intercessory function of the spiritual father or mother is also that of *mesites*, or mediator, defined by Climacus and Symeon as one who "reconciles" the sinner to God. Step One of St. John Climacus:

> All of us who wish to depart from Egypt and to escape Pharaoh certainly need some Moses, as a mediator with God, yet below God, who will stand on our behalf between action and contemplation and lift up his hands to God, so that those under his guidance may cross the sea of sins and overthrow the Amalek of the passions.[3]

Jesus Christ is the ultimate intercessor and mediator between human beings and God the Father, the Source of All. The Holy Ghost is the mediator that brings us to Christ.

Finally, sponsorship or *anadochos* is a culmination of all that the spiritual father gives to his or her disciple. Doctor/healer, teacher,

---

3. Climacus, *The Ladder of Divine Ascent*, Classics of the Contemplative Life (New York: Harper, 1959), Scala 1.

counselor, intercessor, mediator—the sponsor takes the responsibility, safety, and ultimately the salvation of the protégé under his or her care. The sponsor, in effect, takes on the sins, temptations, guilt, worry, and burdens of his charge. In the words of Paul, the spiritual father's job is to "[b]ear one another's burdens and so fulfill the law of Christ" (Gal. 6:2). According to Ware, there is also reference to the role of counselor as well as confessor in the *Apopthegmata*: "'Confess your sin to me and I will carry it,' says Abba Lot to a brother who cannot find peace in his conscience."[4]

SILENCE

Sister Josefina Giosanu, abbess of Văratec Monastery in the region of Neamt, Romania, agrees that nuns also find God and everlasting life in *hesychia*: in silence and in the prayer of solitude, working with a spiritual guide, and by connecting prayer and worship with one's occupation. To pray and then to find silence is the first condition of becoming a nun, but ordinary people can also do it. It is sometimes difficult to find a spiritual guide or mentor, so in the meantime, one can simply take time to pray in connection with one's daily activities.

At Văratec Monastery, the nuns do not pray in the manner of *hesychasm* as practiced on Mt. Athos. Rather, the Jesus Prayer is employed during all activities: daily "office" in their individual cells, then Eucharist in church, then in occupational activities that support the community.

She recommends to both novice nuns and laypersons that the first step to communion with God is to find time for silence—at least a few minutes per day. Uniting with the presence of God in prayerful silence, to the abbess, is like being in the arms of one's parents. "A child keeps quiet when he or she feels the arms of his/her parents and feels the joy of being with her parents. I think it is the same feeling when a novice comes and when she finds silence. When she finds herself in such an environment she feels the love of God."[5] This is possible for

---

4. Kallistos Ware in Irénée Hausherr, *Spiritual Direction in the Ancient Christian East*, Cistercian Studies Series (Kalamazoo, MI: Cistercian Publications, 1989), xxi–xxii.

5. Recorded January 24, 2007, Bucovina, Baia Mare, Romania. HD Master Reel 36-2.

those outside convents as well. It is a good image to adopt when one is attempting to find moments of silence.

Silence is difficult, she warns. It is a balance between "what to do and when to keep silent." Once silence is found, even for a moment, it is useful to then connect it to prayer, or to whatever work one is engaged in.

Silence has to be learned; it is not something that happens, or is simply willed, or the result of being shy or humble. It is difficult for the nun, and it is difficult for people "in the world."

> I think that the powerful aspect of the inner life, and finding your peace, your inner piece . . . can be achieved both in the world and in the monastery. All the laypeople too, should not believe that it is much more difficult for them to find inner peace if they keep strong contact with the church. We know that everyone has his own thoughts and temptations of the world, but if somebody gets into a church and stops in front of an icon and starts concentrating and trying to be alone for seconds, at least for seconds with God, that will help him or her concentrate, gather, or bring together all the thoughts and that gives the power to find peace and continue on, in getting further on.[6]

A REGULAR ROUTINE OF PRAYER

Sister Josefina Giosanu says, too, that action and work are also an essential and inseparable part of their practice of silence and prayer at Văratec. The combination of silence, church attendance, work, and prayer are the ways in which anyone can begin a practice of *hesychia*.

There is a tradition of recitation of the psalms, not only as part of the liturgical celebration but also during the course of daily activities. Monks were to memorize all 150 psalms and to repeat them on schedules: all in one day, or in one week combined with regular duties. McGuckin writes, "Reciting the psalms in the common church was one thing; but the monks were also instructed in how to use the psalm verses in private prayer too: and this was a significantly different

6. Ibid. HD Master Reel 36–4.

style of praying. It has been called 'Monologistic Prayer' and was seen widely as an important technique for focusing the heart and soul, and preparing them for spiritual stillness (*Hesychia*); that important precondition for being able to hear the voice of God in prayer (as distinct from drowning out God's voice by the uninterrupted chatter of our own prayers)."[7] This continual prayer, in silence or in soft voice, was described by the Greek word *mystikos*, also the root of the English word *mystical*. McGuckin further notes that this is the first citation of the word in the Christian vocabulary.

FINDING INNER PEACE

Hesychia and finding inner peace is of vital importance to the *geron*, Elder Pavlos, current spiritual father of St. Catherine's Monastery. He teaches that "[t]he church prays first for the inner peace to come to its members and then to the whole world. St. Dorotheos writes in his ascetic works that peace of the soul is half of the spiritual life: in other words, if a person loses the peace of his soul, he has lost half of his spiritual life."[8]

I asked the elder how one should go about finding and maintaining the peace of the soul. He explained that first the monk or layperson needs to go through a period of cleansing and purification. This is reminiscent of the work taught by centuries of the Desert Fathers under the process of *apatheia*, coming from Hellenic philosophy, then the Neoplatonists, to Paul, Origen, Evagrius, and the Cappadocians onward. Elder Pavlos keeps the process alive and relevant in a contemporary context:

> The basic purpose is to struggle to cleanse the heart from sin. Because when there is sin there's also agitation/trouble/disturbance in the person. The more he advances in virtue and cuts the passions, then the peace of the soul comes as a fruit of his struggles. St. John [Climacus] says in his book that at one time he went to a hut, which housed a

---

7. John Anthony McGuckin, "Prayer of the Heart," unpublished, 2007. Courtesy of the author.

8. Recorded January 16, 2007, Mt. Sinai. HD Master Reel 10.

few ascetics, and from the outside he heard commotion/ disturbance. Then he opened the door and told the group of ascetics, "How will the desert be of benefit to you? You're better off returning to the world." In other words, if a person is not careful, even if he lives in the desert, he will lose his peace. And vice versa, if a person is careful, even if he lives in the world, he will maintain this peace.[9]

Meyendorff claims "it is the special task of Eastern Orthodox spirituality to make known to us the presence of God in history, and to make this known not only in words but also providing living examples of God's power. God is henceforth present in the Church not only in His written Word, but in the reality of the sacraments and in the gifts of the Spirit, evident in His saints, which are available likewise to all Christians who are determined to live in accordance with their baptismal promises." This gift from God comes individually and internally, and also publicly, though the liturgy.

Elder Pavlos loves the liturgy, "God of course has honored us with the office of the priesthood and we liturgize: it is a feeling which cannot be described in words, the joy that the priest feels during the Divine Liturgy. The faithful person also feels this joy during his prayer."

THE PEACE OF *HESYCHIA* AND THE LOVE OF GOD INDEPENDENT OF TIME OR PLACE OR POSITION IN LIFE

Bishop Kallistos Ware counsels, "A man may accomplish the visible and geographic flight into the desert and in his heart still remain in the midst of the city; conversely, a man may continue physically in the city and yet be a true *hesychast* in his heart. What matters is not the Christian's spatial position but one's spiritual state."

St. Isaac the Syrian insisted that inward *hesychia* was impossible without external solitude, but there are many examples of people living outside deserts and monasteries who were practicing *hesychia* while being active in the world, as noted in *Sayings of the Desert Fathers*.

9. Ibid.

An Alexandrian medical doctor is compared to St. Antony. A disciple of St. Gregory of Sinai was refused tonsure and sent back to live on Mt. Athos, then in the city of Thessalonika to instruct lay students in the art. Ware states, "Gregory could scarcely have done this had he regarded the vocation of an urban hesychast as impossible." And Athonite St. Gregory Palamas insisted that Paul's exhortation to "pray without ceasing" (1 Thess. 5:17) was intended for all Christians, not just monks in caves or monasteries.[10] St. Symeon the New Theologian found that God's presence is to be found "in the middle of cities," and "in mountains and cells." Married persons are also able to practice prayer and contemplation: St. Peter had a mother-in-law, yet he was called to climb Mt. Tabor and experience the wonders of the Transfiguration.[11]

It is also possible to do a great deal of talking and also keep silent and contemplative, like those who have jobs helping others, such as guides in monasteries who greet visitors, or the clergy who speak from morning until night and then keep silent vigil and prayer. A way of speaking all day, saying nothing except what is helpful to others or to spread the gospel, is also in keeping with the practices of stillness and silence. We met many of these types of *hesychasts* in Egypt at St. Catherine's and St. Antony's monasteries, Vatopedi on Mt. Athos, and in Romania particularly at Voronet, Rohia, and Agapia.

The words they utter to visitors come from their love of God in silence and prayer.

The peace and love that are found in these holy and ancient places can be found anywhere, because God is all in all, in everything and in everyone.

---

10. Thomas Merton, *Merton and Hesychasm: The Prayer of the Heart*, ed. Bernadette Dieker and Jonathan Montaldo, the Fons Vitae Thomas Merton Series (Louisville: Fons Vitae, 2003), 22.

11. Ibid.

Conclusion

It is a primary and natural human desire to seek peace and tranquility and to be united with God, our Creator. This is *hesychia*, a primal state of union with God.

From nothingness, God materializes and breathes into us his miraculous gift of life. From nonliving matter, God forms us into living human beings. As much as we want to live, we also want to enjoy that original state of peace and purity, to be freed from the emptiness of worldly possessions and false images. We want to find meaning and purpose in our lives, and we want to manifest the truth of our existence.

From the silence, stillness, and safety of our mother's womb we are born into a world that is endlessly vibrating with stimuli. From the second we arrive on this earth our senses come alive with multitudes of sounds, images, lights, colors, and sensations of hot, cold, soft, hard, rough, and smooth. We breathe our first breath of air that fills our lungs and gives us life. We inhale oxygen, but also pollutants and toxins. We taste the nutrients in our mother's milk. Then as we grow we drink water, the liquid of life, and then a variety of other tastes, good and bad.

From silence and stillness, our Creator forms us from inert material and brings us to life in a seemingly limitless variety of worldly experiences and activities. The problem is that many think these experiences and materiality are the best that life has to offer.

This noisy cycle of birth, activity, and death is the natural phenomenon of the human condition. The longing for peace and stillness; the craving for connection with others; the hunger for reunion with our creator God is also universally human.

However, the mystery of creation is that the Creator is present inside, behind, above, and below what he has created! There is no separation between God and creation. This is a major tenet of Orthodox teachings. This means he is also present in each of us.

If we make the worldly things of creation a priority, we miss the subtlety of the Creator. Therefore, to sense the image of God in us, to completely realize and experience that we are created in his likeness, a diminution of stimuli is also required. Remove the material and the worldly and become completely silent and still, and God the Father is there, awaiting us. Through his grace, divinity is revealed within us.

Removal of stimuli, and learning to not be deceived by material splendor is the practice of *hesychia*. It is a method of removal from illusion and dependence on outside factors. Stilling the mind of random thoughts (*logismoi*) allows us a space for God to enter our intellect, and then flow into our heart and soul (*nous*). By remaining still, limiting physical activity and the myriad desires of the body (through the practice of *apatheia*), we also feel God's grace in a physical way; we are gifted by grace to realize that we are the embodiment of God.

We need silence in order to hear God. We also need places of quiet and stillness, where we can contemplate God and pray. Yet few of the readers of this book can or would wish to leave all behind and enter a monastic life. Not many people have the possibility or desire to give away all possessions, leave work, families, and colleagues and take on the ascetic life. To practice *hesychia* or *hesychasm* in the way that Orthodox monks and nuns do for many hours of the day and night, getting very little sleep and in constant prayer, may actually be harmful to the layperson or those working without a seasoned Spiritual Father or Mother to guide them. Many ancient and contemporary texts and several practitioners in this project caution against attempting a full-time practice of *hesychia* alone, or outside a monastery or convent.

Finding a place and time to practice moments of *hesychia* is quite possible and advisable. One does not need to live in a cave, desert, or faraway forest in order to become attuned to God. In a crowded city one could simply visit a library. One could also visit a church for a few moments of prayer, or recitation of the name of Jesus while looking at the cross on an altar or an icon may be helpful. Attending vespers, matins, or a Holy Eucharist service, whether one is a chrismated Orthodox member or not, may offer great peace and healing. Another method might be to share community at a church coffee hour or meals after church services. Any number of these methods may be effective in gaining spiritual fellowship and enjoying moments of spiritual peace and communion with God.

A quiet sanctuary in one's home, a corner of a bedroom or living room, may suffice. Create an altar in a corner of this sanctuary with a candle and a picture of Jesus Christ and/or a saint. Light a stick of incense to invoke a perfect environment for spiritual connection, symbolizing both a gift to God and the presence of the Holy Spirit. A minute of silence and reflection before eating a meal may also be considered *hesychia*.

Thinking of God, saying the Jesus Prayer for five to ten minutes in the morning, afternoon, and evening and tying it to inhalation and exhalation is a form of *hesychasm.* It may be helpful to integrate the Jesus Prayer into one's work and recite it before beginning a new task, or after completing work. Silently repeating Jesus' name every time one sees another person is a way of prayer.

More and more corporations are offering rooms for nondenominational worship and contemplation. Even at work one may still take time to be silent at one's desk or to utter a silent prayer before or during a business meeting. Taking a prayer-walk at lunchtime, uniting one's steps with the Jesus Prayer may bring a deep sense of peace. This practice of *hesychia* at the office may be significantly helpful in improving concentration and mood. Major airports now have nondenominational rooms set aside for introspection and spiritual pause. Even shopping malls have areas of quiet, with trees, flowers, and patches of green grass in which to enjoy a tiny piece of nature and peacefulness. Public parks can be perfect havens of silence and stillness.

One can use ancient and new media to practice *hesychia*. Reading ancient texts like St. John Climacus's *The Ladder of Divine Ascent, The Philokalia*, or the *Apophthegmata Patrum* (*Sayings of the Desert Fathers*) may offer a way to begin a practice of *hesychia*. There is a treasury of new books available for scholars and laypersons. Collections of ancient source material have been translated into many languages, anthologies, and secondary analytical texts.

The medium of film and television, such as the documentary video as a companion to this book, is a way of learning about or initiating a practice. It was my intention in making the ethnographic film to offer explanations and demonstrations of *hesychia* and *hesychasm* that have not been previously available. I hope that by watching this DVD, the reader and viewer may be persuaded to try prayer and contemplation or attend a church service or visit a monastery. It is also my hope that the video itself may create a feeling of peace or connection with God while watching it. There are other films made about monks and nuns in monasteries, such as the recent *Into Great Silence* (Zeitgeist Films, 2006) about Carthusian monks in the French Alps, *Inside Mt. Athos* (BBC, 1970), *Frontline: The Early Christians* (WGBH/PBS, 2000), *Mt. Athos: Mountain of Silence* (Ministry of Hellenic Culture, 1989), but none that actually demonstrate or discuss the practices by the practitioners themselves, and they say nothing specifically about *hesychia*. Yet these films have brought a sense of peace and have helped open the monastery doors, so to speak, paving the way for the monks and nuns to finally break their silence. The *hesychasts*, at least those interviewed in this book, now realize the power of screen media to convey messages of peace, allowing their prayers for the world to be amplified and extended.

There are also new, alternative ways to attain fellowship and connection with the sacred via the Internet. Many websites now exist that offer written texts, audio, video, meditation guides, and even online worship. A major presence on the Internet is www.Beliefnet.com, which has over 25 million users per month.[1] Also, the Greek Orthodox Church of America has much material on *hesychia*, Orthodox worship, and online church services at www.goarch.org. The Orthodox Church of America (OCA) has similar offerings at www.oca.org. Most of the monasteries in this book, however, have no websites as they do not want to be publicly known or encourage visitors. However, many commercial travel companies and guides provide information about them. Quite a

---

1. For the purpose of full disclosure, I need to mention that I had been a columnist and contributing editor on Beliefnet since the website started in 1998, through 2011. Some of the material in this book was adapted for their website, prior to my writing this book. At the time, Beliefnet.com was owned by Fox Digital, a division of Rupert Murdoch's News Corporation.

number of monasteries in America and England have their own websites and offer hospitality to "pilgrims" who are spiritual seekers. An encyclopedia of Christian Orthodoxy can be found online, which offers some information at www.orthodoxwiki.org, but as it is user generated and uncurated, it cannot be considered a reliable academic reference. There are tens of thousands of websites that offer books, icons, music, vestments, and a vast amount of church information of varying quality and relevance.

Ultimately it is paradoxical to write words on the subject of silence and to attempt to describe indescribable experiences. Recording the actions and experiences of the monks and nuns on the subject of stillness is a striking and extreme counterpoint to silence.

It is a grand paradox to discover the peace and joy of silence and stillness—practices involving the absence of stimuli—in Byzantine-influenced Christian Orthodox churches that are overflowing with much stimuli in the form of icons, words, chants, music, fragrances of thick incense, paintings, and mosaics covering every square centimeter of church walls, ceilings, and floors, inside and outside.

I have learned much about the presence and communion with God through this research study. Yet the glory of God and his infinite presence within the cycle of life's activity still remains a mystery.

Appendix 1: Glossary of Terms

Abbess – (Latin, *abbatissa*) Earliest known use is in a sepulchral inscription, 514, on the site of an ancient convent near the basilica of St. Agnes extra muros at Rome. Greek, *hegumene*. Head of a nunnery.[1] Superior of houses of nuns. Depending on the constitution of the convent or house, an abbess may hold office for a term of years, for an indefinite period, until a certain retiring age, and sometimes for life.[2]

Abbot – (Greek, *Patrem*, from Aramaic and Syriac, *abba*, i.e., father) According to the *Rule of St. Benedict*, the abbot is to be regarded as the father of his monastic family. Abbots are always elected and hold authority in accordance with the constitutions of their Order or congregation: sometimes for life, an indefinite term, until reaching a certain age, or for a term of years.[3]

Anaphora – Offering of the liturgical Gifts for consecration. The most important part of the Orthodox Liturgy.[4]

Anchorite (m.) **Anchoress** (f.) – (from Greek, "to withdraw") A person who withdraws from the world to live a solitary life of silence, prayer, and mortification. Technically the term connotes *coenobites* as well as hermits, but is commonly restricted to the latter, i.e., persons who live entirely alone.[5]

---

1. Carolyn L. Connor, *Women of Byzantium* (New Haven: Yale University Press, 2004), 369.

2. *Oxford Dictionary of the Christian Church*, ed. F. L. Cross and E. L. Livingstone, 3rd ed. (New York: Oxford University Press, 1997).

3. Ibid., 2.

4. Nicon D. Patrinacos, *A Dictionary of Greek Orthodoxy = [Lexikon Hellenikes Orthodoxias]* (Pleasantville, NY: Hellenic Heritage Publications, 1984), 20.

Antiphons – Something sung alternatively by two choirs or two cantors.[6]

Apatheia – A habitual state of dispassion, achieved by practicing simplicity, frugality, and solitude according to Evagrius.

Apophatic Theology – "Apophatic theology is a method of theologizing which safeguards the absolute transcendence of God against misrepresentation based upon human analogies."[7] Negative terminology used in Eastern Christian discourse already in use since the fourth century, already a part of the Greek philosophical tradition, found in the *Enneads* of Plotinus (third century). The Cappadocians used it against Eunomios's claim that God's essence may be known. Also in Evagrius (fourth c.) and Dionysius the Aereopagite (sixth c.), "the pre-eminent path of contemplative travel to reach a state of pure prayer."[8]

Apostle – The name has from ancient times signified someone sent by another to carry out an order, a mission, or to transmit a message. In Christianity, the "Twelve Disciples of Christ."[9]

Archbishop – A title signifying the first among bishops, or the chief. It could be an honorary title or one that represents definitive rights and authority in the church.[10]

Archimandrite – In ancient times considered the presiding monk of a large monastery, or the authority of a supervisor of a number of monastic communities. In modern practice, the title is designated for

5. *Oxford Dictionary of the Christian Church*, 59.

6. Patrinacos, *A Dictionary of Greek Orthodoxy = [Lexikon Hellenikes Orthodoxias]*, 32.

7. *The Blackwell Dictionary of Eastern Christianity*, 36.

8. Vladimir Lossky, *The Mystical Theology of the Eastern Church* (Crestwood, NY: St. Vladimir's Seminary Press, 1976).

9. Patrinacos, *A Dictionary of Greek Orthodoxy = [Lexikon Hellenikes Orthodoxias]*, 34.

10. Ibid., 39.

celibate priests in administrative positions. Ranked immediately below the bishop.[11]

Asceticism, *Ascesis* – Nineteenth century, Greek, *askesis*, or "training," from *askein*, "to exercise." Used by Greek philosophers to imply moral training, or voluntary abstention from certain pleasures; (1) practices employed to combat vices and develop virtues, (2) renunciation of various facets of customary social life and comfort or the adoption of painful conditions for religious reasons.[12]

Athonites – Monks who live on the Holy Mountain, Mount Athos in Greece.

Baptism – Sacramental initiation into the Christian church. First of seven sacraments without which membership in the Orthodox Church cannot be held. "Christ Himself pointed out the necessity of a spiritual regeneration by way of 'water and the Spirit' (John 3:5), thus instituting the sacrament of baptism."[13]

Beatitude – The total and ultimate perfection of a human being, blessed by grace in the supernatural order: "the beatific vision, the resurrection of the flesh, the definitive *basileia* of God (Heaven), in the perfected communion of saints Eschatology)."[14]

Bishop – The English term is an Anglo-Saxon corruption of the term "episcopus," which is a transliteration of the original Greek term *episcopos*.[15] The highest rank of the Christian priesthood.

Canonization or Canonized – Differing from the Roman Catholic, in Orthodoxy it is "the allowance of tradition and public veneration

---

11. Ibid., 40.

12. *Oxford Dictionary of the Christian Church*, 113.

13. Patrinacos, *A Dictionary of Greek Orthodoxy = [Lexikon Hellenikes Orthodoxias]*, 45.

14. *Dictionary of Theology*, ed. Karl Rahner and Herbert Vorgrimler, 2nd ed. (New York: Crossroad, 1981), 43–44.

15. Patrinacos, *A Dictionary of Greek Orthodoxy = [Lexikon Hellenikes Orthodoxias]*, 57.

to finally make the selection to sainthood . . . the way by which approval of the Church was and is expressed for a particular saint is by composing for him/her a liturgical service, by setting aside a particular day in the year for his/her veneration, by venerating his/her relics, if extant, by depicting him/her on icons for public veneration, and by erecting to his/her memory places of public worship, that is churches."[16]

Cell – Private room or apartment of a religious person of either sex. A hermit's cell leading an eremitical life. (2) A monastic house dependent on a mother house, in control of its personnel and property. (3) Small groups of Christians, mainly laypeople pledged to intensive work for prayer, study, service, counsel, etc.[17]

Church – From the Greek *kyriakon*, meaning something that belongs to the Lord. In German, *kirche*, in Dutch *kerke*. The word was originally applied to a building. It may also signify an assembly of citizens of a self-governing city. It is also considered by many to be "the body of Christ" with a membership of Christians participating in baptism, chrismation, and Holy Communion.[18]

Coenobitic – Greek, "living in a community," from "common," "life," "way of life." A monk or nun who has taken vows, who lives in community, either in separate dwellings and observes rules of silence, or lives in a common household or building.[19]

Coinherence – The Trinity is of one essence, eternal and unchanging, and all three aspects, Father, Son, and Holy Spirit, are all from the Father.

---

16. Ibid., 69.

17. *Oxford Dictionary of the Christian Church*, 311.

18. Patrinacos, *A Dictionary of Greek Orthodoxy = [Lexikon Hellenikes Orthodoxias]*, 88.

19. *Oxford Dictionary of the Christian Church*, 373.

Desert – Has its origins in Latin: *desertum*, "something left waste," from *deserere*, to "leave, forsake."[20] The Greeks have a word for desert, *eremos*, which means "abandonment." The word *hermit* is a derivation.

Diatiposeis – Ontological appraisals, of our own imagination.

Dualism – (1) Doctrine that holds that mind and matter are distinct and separate, equally real; opposite of monism, that all that exists has a singular nature. (2) A metaphysical system: good and evil are the outcome or product of ultimate first causes. (3) The Nestorian view that in the Incarnate Christ there were not only two natures, but two persons, human and divine.[21]

Ekstasis – (Greek: displacement, cession, trance, ecstasy) The state of being outside of oneself, or separation of the soul from the body; mystical or prophetic bliss, or rapture.

Elder – A church officer, either a teacher or administrator. Cf. Tim. 5:17.

Energies – (Greek *energeiai*) "The principle is that God's essence (*ousia*) is distinct from his energies or activities in the world, and it is the energies that enable us to experience something of the Divine. These energies are 'unbegotten' or 'uncreated.' These energies cannot be created or destroyed . . ." [22]Most famously formulated by St. Gregory Palamas, defending *hesychast* practice involving the vision of a "Divine Light" against charges of heresy brought by Barlaam of Calabria.

Eremitic – The solitary life, or life as a hermit.

---

20. Compact Oxford English Dictionary of Current English, ed. Catherine Soanes and Sara Hawker (New York: Oxford University Press, 2005).

21. *Oxford Dictionary of the Christian Church*, 510.

22. St. Gregory Palamas, *The One Hundred and Fifty Chapters*, trans. Robert E. Sinkewicz (Toronto: Pontifical Institute of Mediaeval Studies, 1988), 23.

Eschatology – Theological doctrine of the last things: death, judgment, heaven and hell. The future of things to come, to be revealed to believers. "In present-day theology, 'eschatological' applies to the present insofar as the last days have begun in Christ ('God's eschatological action'); where it seems to refer to the future alone, it means the future as interpreting the present ('eschatological statements of Scripture')."[23]

Essence – The true core of God; indescribable, and may not be understood or experienced by human beings. "Human beings are confined . . . to a particular sphere of spatio-temporal reality. Herein lies the essential distinction between Spirit and anything material."[24]

Eucharist – (Greek: thanksgiving) Instituted by Christ giving thanks (1 Cor. 11:24; Matt. 26:27); or the service as the supreme act of Christian gratitude. Also known in the Eastern Church as "The Divine Liturgy." Early instances of use in the *Didache*, St. Ignatius, St. Justin, St. Paul, and the Synoptic Gospels. The Body and Blood of Christ, in the Eastern Church the symbols or "antitypes" of bread and wine, become the real Presence of God in his Gifts. Also considered sacrificial elements.[25]

Geron **or** *Geronta* – Spiritual master of a Greek monastery or convent. Similar to "elder," or very senior monk or nun with special spiritual wisdom and insight.

Gnosis – Knowledge.

God – ". . . the word used as a common noun, as in polytheism, where a number of supposed existences claim belief, worship, and service, and as a proper name, e.g. in monotheism, where there is and can be but one such existence. Judaism, Islam and Christianity all proclaim belief in one God. Christianity alone affirms that God is a trinity in unity,

---

23. *Dictionary of Theology*, 153.
24. Ibid., 152.
25. *Oxford Dictionary of the Christian Church*, 685.

a 'Tri-unity', consisting of 'three persons in one substance', the Father being the Source of all existence, the Son the Eternal Object of the Father's love and the mediator of that love in creation and redemption, and the Holy Spirit the bond of Union between the Father and the Son."[26]

Harmolypi (**joyful sorrow**) – As His Eminence Archbishop Damianos puts it, *harmolypi* is a feeling of simultaneous joy and regret when faced with the awe of an encounter with God, and the sorrow for one's sins.

Hermit – An individual who for religious or spiritual reasons has retired into a life of solitude. Originally applied to Christian hermits in Egypt in the third century. "In the Eastern Church . . . hermits still exist; they observe no uniform rule of life and though some live in isolation, others unite in loosely organized communities which sometimes develop into monasteries proper."[27]

Hesychasm – (Greek, quietness) A tradition of a type of prayer methodology employing contemplative silence and stillness such as the Jesus Prayer linked to breathing and postures. In the Eastern and Greek Orthodox churches; mystical, tied to monks on Mount Athos. Originates in the second century with St. Antony, then in the fourth to fifth centuries with St. Gregory of Nyssa, Evagrius, Diadochus, et al. Later, other monks and theologians used the term: St. John Climacus, St. Maximus the Confessor, and St. Symeon the New Theologian. The "physical method" from Athonites St. Gregory Palamas and St. Gregory of Sinai was centered on the union of the mind and the heart. They taught that breathing should be "carefully controlled so as to keep time with recitation of the prayer"—head bowed, eyes fixed to the heart. "This prayer of the heart leads eventually, in those who are specially chosen by God, to the vision of the Divine Light, which, it was believed, can be seen—with the material eyes of the body, although it is first necessary for a man's physical faculties to be refined by God's grace and so rendered spiritual . . . hesychasts believed this

26. Ibid.
27. Patrinacos, *A Dictionary of Greek Orthodoxy* = *[Lexikon Hellenikes Orthodoxias]*, 192.

Light to be identical with the Light that surrounded the Lord at His
Transfiguration on Mt. Tabor, and to be none other than the uncreated
energies of the Godhead."[28]

Hesychast – A practitioner of *hesychia*.

Hesychazo – Withdrawal.

Hesychia – ("silence," "quietude") Internal state of soul, according to
Ware. "It denotes the attitude of one who stands in his heart before
God." (1) A positive method of silence, stillness, and prayer, which may
through God's grace (2) instill a state of spiritual connection and peace
in those who practice it.

Holy Mysteries – The Eucharist, or Gifts.

Hypostases – Hypostatic union in other words refers to the "personal"
Incarnation of the Logos, the Second Person of the Trinity.

I.E.D. – Improvised Explosive Device.

Iconostasis – The wall or screen of icons protecting the Holy of Holies
altar area in the apse of a church.

Idiorrhythmic – A community of monks, a lavra, or coenobitic
monastery where everyone is on their own schedule. May or may not
follow specific *Typikons*.

Immanence – Something that does not exceed a limit. A title for a
high-ranking church official.

Jesus Prayer – "Prayer of the heart" (or the Greek variation, *kyrie
eleison*). A short prayer derived from the New Testament or Christian
Bible. The usual contemporary version is "Lord Jesus Christ, Son of
God, have mercy on me [or us], a sinner [sinners]." "For the *hesychast*

---

28. *Oxford Dictionary of the Christian Church*, 763–64.

the prayer plays a central role; the consciousness being carried inward with the breath to the region of the heart, the symbolic centre of life and awareness . . . at one and the same time a device for excluding thought and images and focusing attention, and an act of acknowledgment, orientation, worship, repentance and devotion, opening up the whole person to the transforming grace of Christ present by his Holy Spirit in the depth of his or her own being."[29]

Katastasis – A unity with one's true state of being.

Lavra – A community of monks living separately, but under a single abbot, gathering on Sundays and feast days for the Liturgy. Can also mean a major monastic house. St. Euthymios (d. 473) founded several *lavras* in the fifth century in Palestine. Mt. Athos has the Great Lavra, founded by Athanasios of Trebizond in 963, the oldest on Mt. Athos. There are several cave *lavras* in Kiev, known as the Lavra of the Caves.[30]

Likeness (*homoiosis*) and Image of God – (1) The whole man or woman is created in the image of God (cf. Gen 1:26). (2) The Image of God *simpliciter* is Jesus Christ, the Logos, who makes God visible. (3) One who believes in Jesus Christ becomes the image of the transfigured Lord in this world (2 Cor. 3:18).[31]

Liturgy (of St. John Chrysostom) – "A document now dated as belonging to the eighth to ninth century but for a long time believed to be the work of St. Proclos, Patriarch of Constantinople (d. 446), related that St. Chrysostom appropriated the liturgy bearing the name of St. Basil. Embellished it with certain prayers of his own and introduced it to Constantinople . . . a reshaping and shortening of the Antiochian liturgy."

Logismoi – Thoughts; often distracting thoughts that disturb the mind's attempt at contemplation. Also thought of as anything that takes us

29. *The Blackwell Dictionary of Eastern Christianity*, 268.

30. Ibid., 294.

31. *Dictionary of Theology*, 228.

away from thoughts of Christ; a result of the fall of humankind. St. John Climacus in *The Ladder of Divine Ascent* provides specific instruction to monks on how to go beyond *logismoi*. Kyriacos Markides, in his book *The Mountain of Silence*, speaks with a contemporary monk, Fr. Maximos on Mt. Athos, who makes practical suggestions.

Logos – Greek, "word" or "reason," the Second Person of the Trinity, Jesus Christ. First known in pagan and Jewish thought: Heraclitus (c. 500 bce) described the Logos in a pantheistic manner, as universal reason taking over the world. The Stoics appropriated this thinking. In the Old Testament or Jewish Bible, the medium of communication between God and human, and a source of Divine power. In Hellenistic Judaism, the Logos became an independent *hypostasis*, associated with the figure of wisdom. In the New Testament or Christian Bible, the Logos is found only in John (John 1:1, 14; 1 John 1:1; Rev. 19:13). The Logos is also described as "God from eternity, the Creative Word, who became incarnate in the man, Jesus Christ of Nazareth . . . the Messiah."[32]

Matins – Morning liturgies, often celebration of the Eucharist in monasteries; in Byzantine time, the end of the day.

Messalianism – The Messalians (from the Syriac for "praying group") were a group of mystics, beginning in the fourth century, who were condemned as heretics. They were accused of abandoning the Scriptures and advocating a direct, material connection with God. Ultimately both the Eastern and Western churches denounced their practices.

Metropolitan – A metropolitan bishop, or simply metropolitan, pertains to the diocesan bishop or archbishop.

Monad – The living Logos, the Son, Jesus Christ.

---

32. *Oxford Dictionary of the Christian Church*, 992.

Monastery – Latin, *monasterium* became the English form *minster*, applied to large churches. A housing of monks or nuns. "The modern custom of using the word to describe all religious houses of men and of calling houses of nuns, 'convents,' has no authority behind it."[33]

Monk – *Monk* or *monachos* itself means "single," or "one who is alone." A person who has dedicated his entire life to God. A member of a religious community of men, having undertaken vows of chastity, poverty, and obedience. The term is applied generally to hermits or members of a monastic community, with sole duties of offering praise to God.

Mother Superior – Abbess; *hegumene*; head of a nunnery or convent.[34]

Mystical – "In modern usage, immediate knowledge of Ultimate Reality (whether or not this is called God) by direct personal experience. . . . Protestant theologians, from Luther onwards, have tended to regard mysticism with suspicion. E. Brunner and R. Niebuhr held it to be anti-Christian because of its close link [for some] with Neo-Platonism, which seemed to bring it closer to pagan gnosis than to the Gospel's offer of salvation; others feared dangers of pantheism. . . . Mystical Theology . . . has to do with symbols and ritual leading us beyond intellectual notions of God to a real union with Him in the 'truly mystic darkness of unknowing' (*Mystical Theology*, 1.3); here the height of the 'mystic words' of Scripture is apprehended and the 'mysteries of theology are revealed in silence.' . . . Mystical Theology does not just persuade us, it acts on us (*Letters* 9, 1); in submitting to the effects of the Church's rites, we 'undergo divine things.'"[35]

Nous – Generally, *nous* is mind or intellect in the West; soul, or that which perceives God, in the East. *Nous* may take several meanings: the soul or spiritual aspects of a man (as in St. Isaac the Syrian), as well as the heart, or essence of the soul, (cf. *Philokalia*, vol. 2, pp. 109, 73). It may

33. Ibid., 1102.
34. Connor, *Women of Byzantium*, 373.
35. *Oxford Dictionary of the Christian Church*, 1127.

be portrayed as what is behind, or the core of the soul (St. Didochos, ibid., pp. 79, 88). It is sometimes referred to as the "eye of the soul" (*The Orthodox Faith*, St. John of Damascus, FC vol. 37, p. 236). The nous, or energy of the soul might be called "a power of the soul" (*On the Holy Spirit*, St. Gregory Palamas, pp. 2, 9) "consisting of thoughts and conceptual images" (*On the Hesychasts*, St. Gregory Palamas, p. 410, 3).

Nun – Female ascetic. Member of a religious community, or cloistered group of women who have taken vows of poverty, chastity, and obedience.

Obedience – "Moral virtue which inclines a person to carry out the will of his (or her) lawful superior. . . . Absolute obedience is due only to God. . . . Obedience is enjoined by Christ (Jn. 15:10), who by his perfect obedience unto death (Phil. 2:8, Heb. 5:8) is its supreme example."[36]

Orthodox Church – The original church; also called the Eastern, Greek, or Greco-Russian Church, all sharing the same faith and in communication with one another, all following the authority of the Oecumenical Patriarch of Constantinople.

Ousia – Essence, substance, being. Origen (c. 182–c. 251) used it when he said God is one genus of *ousia* yet three distinct species of *hypostasis*: namely the Father, the Son, and the Holy Spirit.

Parousia – The second coming of Christ. The reappearance of Jesus as judge for the Last Judgment.

Passion – (1) Referring to Christ's redemptive suffering during the last days of his earthly life. In modern times, the Greek *pasch* is commonly applied to the annual commemoration of the Death and Resurrection of Christ. . . . "Some scholars believe that this was based on a false etymology of the Greek verb 'to suffer' so the Greek *Pascha* for *Pasch* was wrongly associated with the verb 'to suffer' and, as a result, both

36. Ibid., 1170.

Good Friday and Easter were celebrated together."[37] (2) Bodily desires and distractions to be mitigated or managed with the practice of *apatheia*.

Pathemata – The body and its desires.

Patriarch – From the biblical, a father or ruler of a family or tribe; the great forefathers of Israel, Abraham, Isaac, and Jacob (cf. Genesis 12–50). Also a title from the sixth century for bishops of the five sees of Christendom: Rome, Alexandria, Antioch, Constantinople, and Jerusalem. Recently, the title is for heads of autocephalous churches in the East.[38]

Philokalia – A Greek title meaning "love of the fine," that became associated with anthologies.[39] The best-known is one compiled by Nikodemos of the Holy Mountain and Makarios of Corinth; an encyclopedic collection of mystical and ascetic texts "seen by the compilers as embodying the *hesychast* tradition. . . . The Philokalia is an invaluable resource book for *hesychasts*, but not a replacement of the direct teaching of a spiritual father or mother. . . . The Greek version . . . contains in its latter part detailed directions for the posture to be adopted in prayer, and the control of the breath. The *hesychast* tradition makes it clear that these practices are inessential and certainly not to be used without the direction of a *starets* or *gerontas* (elder)."[40]

Praxis – Action, physical activity. Practice.

Prayer – A petition to God, or making connection with God.

Repentance – Greek, *metanoia*, the admission of one's sins and looking to God for amendment. Contrition. It often includes sorrow or guilt, or to make penance and penitence. "In Orthodox use, the whole

37. Patrinacos, *A Dictionary of Greek Orthodoxy = [Lexikon Hellenikes Orthodoxias]*, 278.
38. *Oxford Dictionary of the Christian Church*, 1231.
39. *The Blackwell Dictionary of Eastern Christianity*, 378.
40. Ibid., 231.

Christian life, and especially the ascetic and monastic life, is frequently spoken of as repentance: the full fruition of repentance is assimilation to God, deification."[41]

Second Person of the Trinity – Jesus Christ. See "Trinity."

Semandron – Greek, a bar of wood or metal that when hit with a hammer or mallet produces a resonant sound that can be heard from long distances. It is used to announce the beginning of church services. The *semandron* replaced the use of bells, forbidden in Christian communities under Islamic rule. The wooden bar is called a *talanton*, sounding similar to the rhythm in which it is hammered, to-ta-lan-ton, to-ta-lan-ton, awaking the sleepy monk to become attuned to his talents given to him by God. The iron *semandron*, called "the iron," is often used to signal that it is time for specific duties to be performed. The *semandron* was mentioned by St. John Climacus. Be sure to listen for both types in the accompanying video.

Silence – c. 1225, from O.Fr. *silence*, "absence of sound," from L. *silentium*, "a being silent," from *silens*, prp. of *silere*, "be quiet or still," of unknown origin. Replaced O.E. *swige*. The verb (trans.) is attested from 1597, from the noun.[42] I have discovered that true silence, or total absence of sound, does not exist.

Skete – A small hut or primitive building separated from larger communities of monks, often in a forest or mountainside.

Starets or *staretz* – Russian or Eastern European equivalent of Greek *gerontas* (elder). A counselor and guide to monks, nuns, and even laypersons, who listens to confessions and thoughts (*logismoi*). Counsel is offered: perhaps given in the form of silence, scriptural phrases, or even riddles. "Discrimination is essential for eldership. *Starchestvo* is a fundamental element in the central tradition of *hesychasm*. This

---

41. Ibid., 404.

42. Dictionary.com. Online Etymology Dictionary. Douglas Harper, Historian. http://dictionary.reference.com/browse/silence

tradition dates back to the desert fathers and mothers, and received new impetus in the eighteenth century, in the Russian empire and Balkans."[43]

Stillness – Origin: before 1000; ME *stilnesse*, OE *stilnes*. (1) Silence; quiet; hush. (2) The absence of motion.[44] As we live in a universe that is constantly oscillating, there actually is no such thing as true stillness. We may perceive that an object is still but that is an illusion. At some level—perhaps atomic—all matter is moving or vibrating.

Theia Ousia – Divine Substance.

Theophany – A divine appearance, as in a manifestation of God; an epiphany.[45]

Theoria – Theory.

Theosis – Divinization, or deification, or making divine is salvation from sin by participation in the life of God. According to this conception, the life of God, given in Jesus Christ to the believer through the Holy Spirit, is expressed beginning in the struggles of this life, increases in the experience of the believer through the knowledge of God, and is later consummated in the resurrection of the believer when the power of sin and death, having been fully overcome by God's life, will lose hold over the believer forever.[46]

Theotokos, or Mother of God, *Panagia* (most holy). "God-bearer"; referring to the Virgin Mary.[47]

---

43. *The Blackwell Dictionary of Eastern Christianity*, 460.
44. Dictionary.com. Dictionary.com Unabridged (v 1.1). Random House, Inc. http://dictionary.reference.com/browse/stillness
45. Connor, *Women of Byzantium*, 374.
46. Reference.com. http://www.reference.com/browse/wiki/Theosis
47. Connor, *Women of Byzantium*, 374.

Transfiguration – The appearance of the Lord in human, earthly form. Referenced in first three Gospels (Matt. 17:1-13; Mark 9:2-13; Luke 9:28-36). Traditionally located on Mt. Tabor, but some scholars prefer Mt. Hermon, or the Mt. of Olives. A demonstration of Jewish Law and Prophets to the messiahship of Christ; divine acknowledgment of his Sonship, and foreshadowing of his glory in eternity.[48]

Trinity – One God exists in three Persons and one substance, Father, Son, and Holy Ghost. "God is one, yet self-differentiated; the God who reveals Himself to mankind is one God equally in three distinct modes of existence, yet remains one through all eternity."[49]

Typikon – (1) A document setting the rule of life of an ascetic community. (2) A book prescribing the order of services for the liturgical year. (3) A sequence to follow in a liturgical or Eucharist service. Contemporary typikons are from the ancient Typikon of St. Sabas, and the modern Constantinopolitan Typikon published by Protopsaltes George Biolakis.[50]

Uncreated Light or Energies – Communion is not, according to St. Gregory, with "created grace," but with God himself. This is what the experience of the "uncreated energies" means. This stems from the Christological doctrine of "hypostatic union."

Vespers – Evening service. In the Eastern Church, the beginning of the day at sunset (a reference to Jewish customs). The first service of the liturgical day.

Xeniteia – Voluntary exile in one's cell.

48. *Oxford Dictionary of the Christian Church*, 1636.
49. Ibid., 1641.
50. *The Blackwell Dictionary of Eastern Christianity*, 500.

Appendix 2: Chronology of Places Visited and Persons Interviewed for This Book and Ethnographic Film

July 2006 – GREECE: Athens, Thessaloniki, Mt. Athos, Serifos, Meteora

Athens: Professor Vasileios Thermos
Mt. Athos, Vatopedi Monastery: Archimandrite Ephraim, Father Matthew, Father Stavros
Serifos, Monastery of the Taxiarches: Father Makarios
Thessaloniki: Father Spyros and Katerina Tsimouris

January 2007 – EGYPT: Mt. Sinai, Sharm el-Sheikh, El-Zaafarana, Wadi Araba, southern Gaiala Plateau, Cairo

El-Zaafarana, Wadi Araba, foot of the southern Gaiala Plateau, St. Antony's Monastery: His Grace Bishop Yustus, Father Lazarus, Father Ruwais Antony
Mt. Sinai, St. Catherine's Monastery: His Eminence Archbishop Damianos of Sinai, Father Gregory, Father Nilus, Father Pavlos
Cairo, Cathedral of St. Mark: His Beatitude the late Pope Shenouda III of Alexandria, His Eminence Archbishop Youannes of Cairo

ROMANIA / TRANSYLVANIA – Sâmbăta de Sus, Rohia, Vâratec, and Agapia Monasteries, Bucharest, Iasi

Bucharest, Dealul Mitropoliei (Patriarchal Palace and Cathedral): His Beatitude, the Late Patriarch Theoctist

Baia Mare, Sâmbâta de Sus Monastery: His Eminence Bishop Laurenţiu Streza, the late Archimandrite Teofil Pârâian

Maramure, Rohia Monastery: His Eminence Bishop Iustin Sigheteanul, Fr. Dani Dorinel, Fr. Cristian Stefan

Bucovina: His Eminence Archbishop Iustinian Chira Maramureseanul

Neamt, Voroneţ Monastery (Convent): Abbess Sister Irina Pântescu, Sister Johana

Vâratec Monastery (Convent): Stareta Stavrofora Iosefina Giosanu

Agapia Monastery (Convent): Mother Maria, Rev. Prof. Ioan Mihoc, Director St. John of Hozeva Lay Academy

Iasi, Exarhos Three Holy Hierarchs Monastery: His Eminence Daniel Ciobotea, Metropolitan of Moldavia & Bucovina (Now His Beatitude Patriarch Daniel), Abbot Archimandrite Clement Haralam, Fr. Dan Sandu

Bibliography

The Blackwell Dictionary of Eastern Christianity. Edited by Kenneth Parry and John R. Hinnells. Oxford: Blackwell, 1999.

Dictionary of Theology. Edited by Karl Rahner and Herbert Vorgrimler. 2nd ed. New York: Crossroad, 1981.

Oxford Dictionary of the Christian Church. Edited by F. L. Cross and E. L. Livingstone. 3rd ed. New York: Oxford University Press, 1997.

Amis, Robin. *A Different Christianity: Early Christian Esotericism and Modern Thought*, Suny Series in Western Esoteric Traditions. Albany: State University of New York Press, 1995.

Antony. *The Letters of St. Antony the Great*. Translated by Derwas J. Chitty, Fairacres Publication. Oxford: SLG, 1975.

Athanasius. *The Life of Antony and the Letter to Marcellinus*. Translated by Robert C. Gregg. New York: Paulist, 1980.

———. *The Life of Antony*. Translated by Tim Vivian, Apostolos N. Athanassakis, John Serapion, Rowan A. Greer, and Benedicta Ward, Cistercian Studies Series. Kalamazoo, MI: Cistercian Publications, 2003.

Athanasius, Pseudo. *The Life of the Blessed & Holy Syncletica*. Translated by Elizabeth Bryson Bongie. Edited by Mary Schaffer. Reprint ed. 2 vols., Peregrina Translations Series. Eugene, OR: Wipf & Stock, 2003.

Athanassakis, Apostolos N. *The Life of Pachomius: Vita Prima Graeca*. 7 vols., Society of Biblical Literature. Texts and Translations, Early Christian Literature Series, Vol. 2. Missoula, MT: Scholars Press for the Society of Biblical Literature, 1975.

Banks, Marcus, and Howard Morphy. *Rethinking Visual Anthropology*. New Haven: Yale University Press, 1997.

Barsanuphius. *Letters from the Desert: A Selection of Questions and Responses*. Translated by John Chryssavgis, St. Vladimir's Seminary Press "Popular Patristics" Series. Crestwood, NY: St. Vladimir's Seminary Press, 2003.

Basil, Saint. *The Ascetic Works of Saint Basil.* Cambridge: University of Cambridge Press, 1925.

———. *Ascetical Works.* Translated by M. Monica Wagner, Fathers of the Church. New York: Fathers of the Church, 1950.

———. *Letters.* Translated by Sister Agnes Clare Way. 2 vols. Vol. 13, Fathers of the Church. New York: Fathers of the Church, 1951.

———. *Exegetic Homilies.* Translated by Agnes Clare Way, Fathers of the Church. Washington, DC: Catholic University of America Press, 1963.

Basil, Saint, Saint Gregory of Nazianzus, and Saint Gregory of Nyssa. *The Fathers Speak: St Basil the Great, St Gregory of Nazianzus, St Gregory of Nyssa.* Translated by Georges Augustin Barrois. Crestwood, NY: St. Vladimir's Seminary Press, 1986.

Bradshaw, Paul F. *The Search for the Origins of Christian Worship: Sources and Methods for the Study of Early Liturgy.* New York: Oxford University Press, 1992.

Brown, Peter Robert Lamont. *The Body and Society: Men, Women, and Sexual Renunciation in Early Christianity,* Lectures on the History of Religions. New York: Columbia University Press, 1988.

Brunner, Emil, and Olive Wyon. *Man in Revolt: A Christian Anthropology.* Philadelphia: Westminster, 1947.

Burton-Christie, Douglas. *The Word in the Desert: Scripture and the Quest for Holiness in Early Christian Monasticism.* New York: Oxford University Press, 1993.

Cabasilas, Nicolaus. *The Life in Christ.* Crestwood, NY: St. Vladimir's Seminary Press, 1974.

Carrette, Jeremy R., and Richard King. *Selling Spirituality: The Silent Takeover of Religion.* New York: Routledge, 2005.

Cassian, John, and Boniface Ramsey. *John Cassian: The Conferences,* Ancient Christian Writers. New York: Paulist, 1997.

———. *John Cassian, the Institutes,* Ancient Christian Writers. New York: Newman, 2000.

Cavarnos, Constantine. *Anchored in God: An Inside Account of Life, Art and Thought on the Holy Mountain of Athos.* Athens: Astir, 1959.

———. *The Holy Mountain: Two Lectures on Mount Athos, of Which the First Deals with Its Scholars, Missionaries, and Saints, and the Second with Its Music, Musicians, and Hymnographers, Together with an Account of a Recent Visit to Athos.* Belmont, MA: Institute for Byzantine and Modern Greek Studies, 1973.

———. *The Hellenic-Christian Philosophical Tradition: Four Lectures Delivered at Boston University.* Belmont, MA: Institute for Byzantine and Modern Greek Studies, 1989.

Chadwick, Owen. *John Cassian.* 2nd ed. London: Cambridge University Press, 1968.

Chitty, Derwas J. *The Desert a City: An Introduction to the Study of Egyptian and Palestinian Monasticism under the Christian Empire.* Crestwood, NY: St. Vladimir's Seminary Press, 1995.

Chryssavgis, John. *Beyond the Shattered Image.* Minneapolis: Light & Life, 1999.

———. *John Climacus: From the Egyptian Desert to the Sinaite Mountain.* Aldershot, UK: Ashgate, 2004.

———. *Light through Darkness: The Orthodox Tradition,* Traditions of Christian Spirituality. London: Darton, Longman & Todd, 2004.

Chryssavgis, John, and Abba Zosimas. *In the Heart of the Desert: The Spirituality of the Desert Fathers and Mothers: With a Translation of Abba Zosimas' Reflections,* Treasures of the World's Religions. Bloomington, IN: World Wisdom, 2003.

Ciobotea, Daniel (Metropolitan and Patriarch). *Confessing the Truth in Love: Orthodox Perceptions on Life, Mission and Unity.* Iasi, Romania: Trinitas, 2001.

Clark, Elizabeth A. *Women in the Early Church,* Message of the Fathers of the Church. Wilmington, DE: Glazier, 1983.

Clement. *Miscellanies.* Translated by Fenton John Anthony Hort and Joseph B. Mayor. Vol. VII. New York: Garland, 1987.

———. *Stromateis.* Translated by John Ferguson. Vol. 1–3, Fathers of the Church. Washington, DC: Catholic University of America Press, 1991.

Climacus, John. *The Ladder of Divine Ascent,* Classics of the Contemplative Life. New York: Harper, 1959.

————. *The Ladder of Divine Ascent*. Translated by Colm Luibhéid and Norman Russell, Classics of Western Spirituality. New York: Paulist, 1982.

Connor, Carolyn L. *Women of Byzantium*. New Haven: Yale University Press, 2004.

Crawford, Peter Ian, and David Turton. *Film as Ethnography*. Manchester, UK: Manchester University Press, St. Martin's Press, 1992.

Dalrymple, William. *From the Holy Mountain: A Journey in the Shadow of Byzantium*. London: HarperCollins, 1997.

Deiss, Lucien. *Early Sources of the Liturgy*. Staten Island, NY: Alba House, 1967.

Diadochus. *Oeuvres Spirituelles: Introduction, Texte Critique*. Translated by Édouard des Places, Sources Chrétiennes; No. 5 Bis. Paris: Cerf, 1955.

Dostoyevsky, Fyodor. "The Brothers Karamazov." NetLibrary, 1976.

Dunn, Marilyn. *The Emergence of Monasticism: From the Desert Fathers to the Early Middle Ages*. Oxford: Blackwell, 2003.

Evagrius. *The Praktikos: Chapters on Prayer*. Translated by John Eudes Bamberger, Cistercian Studies Series. Spencer, MA: Cistercian Publications, 1970.

————. *The Praktikos: Chapters on Prayer*. Translated by John Eudes Bamberger, Cistercian Studies Series. Kalamazoo, MI: Cistercian Publications, 1978.

————. *Sur les Pensées*. Translated by Paul Géhin, Claire Guillaumont, and Antoine Guillaumont, Sources Chrétiennes. Paris: Cerf, 1998.

————. *Evagrius of Pontus: The Greek Ascetic Corpus*. Translated by Robert E. Sinkewicz, Oxford Early Christian Studies. Oxford: Oxford University Press, 2003.

Florovsky, Georges. *Bible, Church, Tradition: An Eastern Orthodox View*. Belmont, MA: Nordland, 1972.

Frend, W. H. C. *The Rise of Christianity*. Philadelphia: Fortress Press, 1984.

Geertz, Clifford. *The Interpretation of Cultures: Selected Essays*. New York: Basic Books, 1973.

Gould, Graham. *The Desert Fathers on Monastic Community*, Oxford Early Christian Studies. Oxford: Oxford University Press, 1993.

Gregory. *Dialogues*. Translated by Odo John Zimmerman. Washington, DC: Catholic University of America Press, 1959.

Gregory of Nazianzus, Saint. *Saint Gregory of Nazianzus: Selected Poems*. Translated by John McGuckin, Fairacres Publication. Oxford: SLG, 1986.

———. *Gregory of Nazianzus, Autobiographical Poems*. Translated by Carolinne White, Cambridge Medieval Classics. New York: Cambridge University Press, 1996.

———. *St. Gregory of Nazianzus: Select Orations*. Translated by Martha Pollard Vinson. Washington, DC: Catholic University of America Press, 2003.

———. *Gregory of Nazianzus: Images and Reflections*. Edited by Jostein Børtnes and Tomas Hägg. Copenhagen: Museum Tusculanum, 2006.

Gregory of Nazianzus, Saint. *Gregory of Nazianzus*. Translated by Brian Daley. London: Routledge, 2006.

Gregory of Nyssa, Saint. *Ascetical Works*. Translated by Virginia Woods Callahan, Fathers of the Church. Washington, DC: Catholic University of America Press, 1967.

———. *The Life of St. Macrina (Vita Sanctae Macrinae)*. Willits, CA: Eastern Orthodox Books, 1975.

———. *The Life of Moses*. Translated by Abraham J. Malherbe and Everett Ferguson, Classics of Western Spirituality. New York: Paulist, 1978.

———. *La Création de l'Homme*. Translated by J. Y. Guillaumin, Collection "Pères dans la Foi." Paris: Desclée de Brouwer, 1982.

———. *On the Soul and the Resurrection*. Translated by Catherine P. Roth. Crestwood, NY: St. Vladimir's Seminary Press, 1993.

———. *Gregory of Nyssa's Treatise on the Inscriptions of the Psalms*. Translated by Ronald E. Heine, Oxford Early Christian Studies. Oxford: Clarendon, 1995.

Gregory Palamas, Saint. *The Triads (Défense des Saints Hésychastes)*. Translated by Nicholas Gendle, Classics of Western Spirituality. New York: Paulist, 1983.

———. *The One Hundred and Fifty Chapters.* Translated by Robert E. Sinkewicz. Toronto: Pontifical Institute of Mediaeval Studies, 1988.

Guy, Jean-Claude. *Les Apophtegmes des Pères: Collection Systématique,* Sources Chrétiennes. Paris: Cerf, 1993.

Harmless, William. *Desert Christians: An Introduction to the Literature of Early Monasticism.* Oxford: Oxford University Press, 2004.

Harper, Ralph. *Journey from Paradise: Mt. Athos and the Interior Life.* Québec: Éditions du Beffroi/Baltimore: Johns Hopkins University Press, 1987.

Hausherr, Irénée. *Hésychasme et Prière,* Orientalia Christiana Analecta. Roma: Pont. Institutum Studiorum, 1966.

———. *The Name of Jesus,* Cistercian Studies Series. Kalamazoo, MI: Cistercian Publications, 1978.

———. *Spiritual Direction in the Ancient Christian East,* Cistercian Studies Series. Kalamazoo, MI: Cistercian Publications, 1989.

Hockings, Paul. *Principles of Visual Anthropology,* World Anthropology. The Hague: Mouton, 1975.

Holmes, Augustine, and Basil. *A Life Pleasing to God: The Spirituality of the Rules of St Basil,* Cistercian Studies Series. Kalamazoo, MI: Cistercian Publications, 2000.

Holy Community of Mount Athos. *Treasures of Mount Athos: Catalogue of the Exhibition.* Edited by Organization for the Cultural Capital of Europe Holy Community of Mount Athos, Athanasios A. Karakatsanis. Thessaloniki, Greece: Ministry of Culture, Museum of Byzantine Culture, 1997.

Irenaeus. *Five Books of S. Irenaeus, Bishop of Lyons, against Heresies.* Oxford: J. Parker, 1872.

Isaac. *The Ascetical Homilies of Saint Isaac the Syrian.* Translated by Holy Transfiguration Monastery. Boston: The Holy Transfiguration Monastery, 1984.

Joanta, Bishop Seraphim. *Romania: Its Hesychast Tradition and Culture.* Translated by Père Romul Joanta (now Bishop Seraphim of Fagaras). Vol. 46, Spiritualité Orientale et Vie Monastique. Wildwood, CA: St. Xenia Skete, 1992.

John Chrysostom, and Jerome. *Jerome, Chrysostom, and Friends: Essays and Translations*. Edited by Elizabeth A. Clark, Studies in Women and Religion. New York: Edwin Mellen, 1979.

John Chrysostom, Saint. *The Homilies of Saint John Chrysostom, Archbishop of Constantinople, on the Epistle of St. Paul the Apostle to the Romans*, Library of Fathers of the Holy Catholic Church. Oxford: J. H. Parker, 1841.

———. *Manual of Christian Doctrine, Comprising Dogma, Moral, and Worship*. 49th ed. Philadelphia: J. J. McVey, 1928.

———. *Selections from St. John Chrysostom*. London: Burns, Oates & Washbourne, 1940. microform.

———. *Sur l'Incompréhensibilité de Dieu*. Translated by Robert Flacelière, Sources Chrétiennes. Paris: Cerf, 1951.

———. *Sur la Providence de Dieu*. Translated by Anne-Marie Malingrey, Sources Chrétiennes. Paris: Cerf, 1961.

———. *Chrysostom and His Message: A Selection from the Sermons of St. John Chrysostom of Antioch and Constantinople*. Translated by Stephen Neill. New York: Association Press, 1963.

———. *Six Books on the Priesthood*. Translated by Graham Neville, a Thoroughly Revised Version of T. A. Moxton's Translation, Published by SPCK in 1907. London: SPCK, 1964.

———. *The Preaching of Chrysostom: Homilies on the Sermon on the Mount*. Edited by Jaroslav Pelikan. Philadelphia: Fortress Press, 1967.

———. *On the Incomprehensible Nature of God*. Translated by Paul W. Harkins, Fathers of the Church. Washington, DC: Catholic University of America Press, 1984.

———. *The Divine Liturgy of Saint John Chrysostom*. Translated by Helenic College/Holy Cross Greek Orthodox School of Theology Faculty. Brookline, MA: Holy Cross Orthodox Press, 1985.

———. *La Divine Liturgie de Saint Jean Chrysostome*. Translated by Danielle Gousseff. Orthodox Eastern Church ed., Catéchèse Orthodoxe. Paris: Cerf, 1986.

———. *Homilies on Genesis 1-17*. Translated by Robert C. Hill. Washington, DC: Catholic University of America Press, 1986.

————. *Trois Catéchèses Baptismales.* Translated by Auguste Piédagnel and Louis Doutreleau, Sources Chrétiennes. Paris: Cerf, 1990.

————. *An Analysis of the Hermeneutics of John Chrysostom's Commentary on Isaiah 1-8 with an English Translation.* Translated by Duane A. Garrett, Studies in the Bible and Early Christianity. Lewiston, NY: Edwin Mellen, 1992.

————. *St. John Chrysostom Commentary on the Psalms.* Translated by Robert C. Hill. 2 vols. Brookline, MA: Holy Cross Orthodox Press, 1998.

Joseph the Hesychast, Elder. *Monastic Wisdom: The Letters of Elder Joseph the Hesychast.* Florence, AZ: Saint Antony's Greek Orthodox Monastery, 1999.

————. *Elder Joseph the Hesychast: Struggles, Experiences, Teachings (1898-1959).* 4th ed. Karyes, Athos, Greece: Great and Holy Monastery of Vatopedi, 1999.

Kaestner, Erhart. *Mount Athos: The Call from Sleep.* Translated by Barry Sullivan. London: Faber & Faber, 1961.

Karakatsanis, Athanasios A., Holy Community of Mount Athos, Organization for the Cultural Capital of Europe. *Treasures of Mount Athos: Catalogue of the Exhibition.* Thessaloniki, Greece: Ministry of Culture, Museum of Byzantine Culture, 1997.

Karambelas, Cherubin. *Recollections of Mount Athos.* Brookline, MA: Holy Cross Orthodox Press, 1987.

Keller, David G. R. *Oasis of Wisdom: The Worlds of the Desert Fathers and Mothers.* Collegeville, MN: Liturgical Press, 2005.

Kontoglou, Photes. *Byzantine Sacred Art: Selected Writings of the Contemporary Greek Icon Painter Fotis Kontoglous on the Sacred Arts According to the Tradition of Eastern Orthodox Christianity.* Translated by Constantine Cavarnos. New York: Vantage, 1957.

Krivocheine, Basil. *In the Light of Christ: Saint Symeon, the New Theologian (949-1022), Life, Spirituality, Doctrine.* Crestwood, NY: St. Vladimir's Seminary Press, 1986.

Lampe, G. W. H. *A Patristic Greek Lexicon.* Oxford: Clarendon, 1961.

Langford-James, R. Ll. *A Dictionary of the Eastern Orthodox Church.* New York: Burt Franklin, 1976.

Loch, Sydney. *Athos: The Holy Mountain.* New York: T. Nelson.

Loizos, Peter. *Innovation in Ethnographic Film: From Innocence to Self-Consciousness, 1955-85.* Chicago: University of Chicago Press, 1993.

Lossky, Vladimir. *The Vision of God.* Translated by Ashleigh Moorhouse. London: Faith Press, 1963.

———. *The Mystical Theology of the Eastern Church.* Crestwood, NY: St. Vladimir's Seminary Press, 1976.

Louth, Andrew. *The Wilderness of God.* London: Darton, Longman & Todd, 1991.

———. *The Origins of the Christian Mystical Tradition: From Plato to Denys.* 2nd ed. Oxford: Oxford University Press, 2007.

Macarius, Pseudo. *Die 50 Geistlichen Homilien des Makarios*, Patristische Texte und Studien. Berlin: De Gruyter, 1964.

———. *The Fifty Spiritual Homilies; and the Great Letter.* Translated by George A. Maloney, Classics of Western Spirituality. New York: Paulist, 1992.

Malaty, Tadros Y. *Introduction to the Coptic Orthodox Church.* Alexandria, Egypt: St. George's Coptic Orthodox Church, 1993.

Man, Grigore. *Biserici de Lemn din Maramures*, Descrierea Cip a Bibliotecii Nationale a Romaniei. Baia Mare: Proem, 2005.

Markides, Kyriacos C. *Gifts of the Desert: The Forgotten Path of Christian Spirituality.* New York: Doubleday/LibraryWeb EBOOKS, 2005.

Maximus. *The Ascetic Life. The Four Centuries on Charity.* Translated by Polycarp Sherwood, Ancient Christian Writers. Westminster, MD: Newman, 1955.

McClellan, Michael W. *Monasticism in Egypt: Images and Words of the Desert Fathers.* Edited by (photographs) Otto Friedrich August Meinardus. Cairo: American University in Cairo Press, 1998.

McGuckin, John Anthony. *At the Lighting of the Lamps: Hymns of the Ancient Church*, Fairacres Publication. Oxford: SLG, 1995.

———. *St. Gregory of Nazianzus: An Intellectual Biography.* Crestwood, NY: St. Vladimir's Seminary Press, 2001.

———. *Standing in God's Holy Fire: The Byzantine Tradition.* London: Darton, Longman & Todd, 2001.

———. *The Book of Mystical Chapters: Meditations on the Soul's Ascent from the Desert Fathers and Other Early Christian Contemplatives.* Boston: Shambhala, 2002.

———. *The Westminster Handbook to Origen,* Westminster Handbooks to Christian Theology. Louisville: Westminster John Knox, 2004.

———. *The Westminster Handbook to Patristic Theology.* Louisville: Westminster John Knox, 2004.

Merrill, Christopher. *Things of the Hidden God: Journeys to the Holy Mountain.* New York: Random House, 2005.

Merton, Thomas. *The Wisdom of the Desert: Sayings from the Desert Fathers of the Fourth Century.* New York: New Directions, 1961.

———. *Merton and Hesychasm: The Prayer of the Heart.* Edited by Bernadette Dieker and Jonathan Montaldo, the Fons Vitae Thomas Merton Series. Louisville: Fons Vitae, 2003.

Meyendorff, John. *A Study of Gregory Palamas.* London and New York: Faith Press/St. Vladimir's Seminary Press, 1964.

———. *Byzantine Theology: Historical Trends and Doctrinal Themes.* New York: Fordham University Press, 1974.

———. *The Orthodox Church: Its Past and Its Role in the World Today.* Crestwood, NY: St. Vladimir's Seminary Press, 1981.

———. *St. Gregory Palamas and Orthodox Spirituality.* Crestwood, NY: St. Vladimir's Seminary Press, 1998.

Migne, J. P. *Patrologia Graeca: Patrologiae Cursus Completus, Seu Bibliotheca Universalis, Integra, Uniformis, Commoda, Oeconomica Omnium Ss Patrum, Doctorum Scriptorumque Ecclesiasticorum,* Graeca. Paris, Parisiorum: http://phoenix.reltech.org/Ebind/docs/Migne/Migne.html, 1857.

———. *Patrologia Latina: The Full Text Database.* Ann Arbor, MI: ProQuest Information and Learning Company: http://www.columbia.edu/cgi-bin/cul/resolve?ANC0798.

Miller, Patricia Cox. *Women in Early Christianity: Translations from Greek Texts.* Washington, DC: Catholic University of America Press, 2005.

Moschus, John. *The Spiritual Meadow (Pratum Spirituale).* Translated by John Wortley. Kalamazoo, MI: Cistercian Publications, 1992.

Mylonas, Paulos M. *Athos and Its Monastic Institutions through Old Engravings and Other Works of Art.* Athens: Printed by I. Makris Papadiamantopoulou, 1963.

———. *Pictorial Dictionary of the Holy Mountain Athos=Bildlexikon des Heiligen Berges Athos.* Tübingen: Wasmuth, 2000.

Nicodemus. *Nicodemos of the Holy Mountain: A Handbook of Spiritual Counsel.* Translated by Peter A. Chambers, Classics of Western Spirituality. New York: Paulist, 1989.

Nicodemus, and Makarios. *The Philokalia: The Complete Text.* Translated by G. E. H. Palmer, Philip Sherrard, and Kallistos Ware. London: Faber & Faber, 1979.

Norwich, John Julius, and Reresby Sitwell. *Mount Athos.* London: Hutchinson, 1966.

Oden, Thomas C. *The Rebirth of Orthodoxy.* New York: HarperSanFrancisco, 2003.

Origen, Paul Koetschau, and G. W. Butterworth. *On First Principles.* Gloucester, MA: P. Smith, 1973.

Paisios, Elder. *Epistles.* Thessaloniki, Greece: Holy Monastery of the Evangelist John the Theologian, 2002.

Palladius. *Palladius: The Lausiac History.* Translated by Robert T. Meyer. Westminster, MD: Newman, 1965.

Papademetriou, George C. *Introduction to St. Gregory Palamas.* Brookline, MA: Holy Cross Orthodox Press, 2004.

Patrinacos, Nicon D. *A Dictionary of Greek Orthodoxy = [Lexikon Hellenikes Orthodoxias].* Pleasantville, NY: Hellenic Heritage Publications, 1984.

Pelekanides, Stylianos M. *The Treasures of Mount Athos: Illuminated Manuscripts, Miniatures-Headpieces-Initial Letters (Hoi Thesauroi Tou Hagiou Orous).* Translated by S. M. Pelekanidis et al. 2 vols. Athens: Ekdotike Athenon, 1974.

Pelikan, Jaroslav. *Christianity and Classical Culture: The Metamorphosis of Natural Theology in the Christian Encounter with Hellenism.* New Haven: Yale University Press, 1993.

Pennington, M. Basil. *O Holy Mountain: Journal of a Retreat on Mount Athos.* Garden City, NY: Doubleday, 1978.

Porphyrios, Elder. *Wounded by Love: The Life and Wisdom of Elder Porphyrios.* Translated by John Raffan. Edited by Sisters of Holy Convent of Chrysopigi. Limni, Evia, Greece: Denise Harvey, 2003.

Prestige, G. L., and F. L. Cross. *God in Patristic Thought.* London: SPCK, 1952.

Prokurat, Michael, Alexander Golitzin, and Michael D. Peterson. *Historical Dictionary of the Orthodox Church.* Lanham, MD: Scarecrow, 1996.

Rachmaninoff, Sergei, Anthony Antolini, and Orthodox Eastern Church. *The Liturgy of St. John Chrysostom.* New York: Galaxy Music Corporation, 1988.

Ruether, Rosemary Radford. *Gregory of Nazianzus, Rhetor and Philosopher.* Oxford: Clarendon, 1969.

Russell, Catherine. *Experimental Ethnography: The Work of Film in the Age of Video.* Durham, NC: Duke University Press, 1999.

Schmemann, Alexander. *Introduction to Liturgical Theology,* Library of Orthodox Theology. London: Faith Press, 1966.

Seraphim, Rose. *The Holy Fathers: Sure Guide to True Christianity.* Edited by Saint Herman of Alaska Brotherhood. Platina, CA: St. Herman Brotherhood, 1983.

Sherrard, Philip. *Athos, the Mountain of Silence.* London and New York: Oxford University Press, 1960.

Sherrard, Philip, and Takis Zervoulakos. *Athos, the Holy Mountain.* Woodstock, NY: Overlook, 1985.

Sofrony, Archimandrite. *The Undistorted Image: Staretz Silouan, 1866-1938.* Translated by Rosemary Edmonds. London: Faith Press, 1958.

———. *The Monk of Mount Athos: Staretz Silouan, 1866-1938.* Translated by Rosemary Edmonds. Revised ed. London: Mowbrays, 1973.

Spencer, Matthew. *Athos: Travels on the Holy Mountain.* London: Azure, 2000.

Symeon the New Theologian, Saint. *Sources Chrétiennes.* Paris: Cerf, 1942.

———. *Catéchèses.* Translated by Joseph Paramelle. Paris: Cerf, 1963.

———. *Symeon the New Theologian: The Discourses*, Classics of Western Spirituality. New York: Paulist, 1980.

———. *The Practical and Theological Chapters & the Three Theological Discourses*. Kalamazoo, MI: Cistercian Publications, 1982.

———. *On the Mystical Life: The Ethical Discourses*. Translated by Alexander Golitzin. 3 vols. Crestwood, NY: St. Vladimir's Seminary Press, 1995.

Taft, Robert F. *A History of the Liturgy of St. John Chrysostom*. Roma: Pont. Institutum Studiorum Orientalium, 1975.

Theophilus, and Gustave Bardy. *Trois Livres à Autolycus*, Sources Chrétiennes. Paris: Cerf, 1948.

Thunberg, Lars. *Microcosm and Mediator: The Theological Anthropology of Maximus the Confessor*. 2nd ed. Chicago: Open Court, 1995.

Treadgold, Warren T. *A History of the Byzantine State and Society*. Stanford, CA: Stanford University Press, 1997.

Turner, Victor Witter, and Edward M. Bruner. *The Anthropology of Experience*. Urbana: University of Illinois Press, 1986.

Valantasis, Richard. *Religions of Late Antiquity in Practice*, Princeton Readings in Religions. Princeton: Princeton University Press, 2000.

Vasileios, Archimandrite. *Hymn of Entry: Liturgy and Life in the Orthodox Church*, Contemporary Greek Theologians. Crestwood, NY: St. Vladimir's Seminary Press, 1984.

Vasileios, Archimandrite, and Georgios Mantzardis. *The Meaning of Typikon*. Translated by Elizabeth Theokritoff. Montréal: Alexander, 1997.

Vivian, Tim. *Journeying into God: Seven Early Monastic Lives*. Minneapolis: Fortress Press, 1996.

Vivian, Tim, and Rowan A. Greer. *Four Desert Fathers: Pambo, Evagrius, Macarius of Egypt, and Macarius of Alexandria; Coptic Texts Relating to the Lausiac History of Palladius*, St. Vladimir's Seminary Press "Popular Patristics" Series. Crestwood, NY: St. Vladimir's Seminary Press, 2004.

Waddell, Helen. *The Desert Fathers: Translations from the Latin with an Introduction*. Ann Arbor: University of Michigan Press, 1957.

Ward, Benedicta. *The Wisdom of the Desert Fathers: The Apophthegmata Patrum (the Anonymous Series)*, Fairacres Publication. Oxford: SLG, 1975.

———. *The Sayings of the Desert Fathers: The Alphabetical Collection*. London: Mowbrays, 1975.

———. *The Desert Christian: Sayings of the Desert Fathers; the Alphabetical Collection*. New York: Macmillan, 1980.

———. *The Desert Fathers: Sayings of the Early Christian Monks*, Penguin Classics. London: Penguin, 2003.

Ware, Kallistos. *The Power of the Name: The Jesus Prayer in Orthodox Spirituality*, Fairacres Publication. Oxford: SLG, 1974.

———. *The Orthodox Way*. Rev. ed. Crestwood, NY: St. Vladimir's Seminary Press, 1998.

Wimbush, Vincent L. *Ascetic Behavior in Greco-Roman Antiquity*, Studies in Antiquity and Christianity. Minneapolis: Fortress Press, 1990.

Wimbush, Vincent L., and Richard Valantasis. *Asceticism*. New York: Oxford University Press, 1995.

Wybrew, Hugh. *The Orthodox Liturgy: The Development of the Eucharistic Liturgy in the Byzantine Rite*. London: SPCK, 1989.

Index

For additional information and materials, please visit
BeStillAndKnow.info.